First Church of Christ

First half-century book of the First Church of Christ

1830-1879

First Church of Christ

First half-century book of the First Church of Christ
1830-1879

ISBN/EAN: 9783337233907

Printed in Europe, USA, Canada, Australia, Japan

Cover: Foto ©Lupo / pixelio.de

More available books at **www.hansebooks.com**

FIRST

HALF-CENTURY BOOK,

1830 — 1879

OF THE

FIRST CHURCH OF CHRIST

— CONGREGATIONAL —

OF ITHACA, N. Y.

PUBLISHED BY ORDER OF THE CHURCH.

Half-Century History.

ON the second day of April of the year eighteen hundred and thirty, the Rev. Jno. F. Schermerhorn, of Utica, Agent of the General Synod of the Protestant Reformed Dutch Church in America, organized the Protestant Reformed Dutch Church of Ithaca. On the same day, Daniel L. Bishop, Isaac Carpenter, and Augustus Sherrill were ordained Elders, and Levi Kirkham and Daniel Pratt, Deacons.

The new church was made up of thirty-one members who had withdrawn by regular dismissal from the Presbyterian church of Ithaca, then under the pastoral care of the Rev. Dr. Wisner, and one member from the Dutch church of Poughkeepsie. The Presbyterian church in the village was large in numbers, and there was more or less of restiveness under Dr. Wisner's somewhat rigid rule.

There had been previous consultation and deliberation, and a meeting had been held to hear the report of a committee raised to inquire into the expediency of forming another Presbyterian, or a Congregational church in the village. At this meeting a letter from the Rev. Isaac Ferris, of Albany, about the forming of a Dutch Church in Ithaca, brought about an unanimous vote, that it was expedient that such a church be formed ; and a committee consisting of Daniel L. Bishop, Cornelius P. Heermans, and Augustus Sherrill, was appointed to confer with Mr. Ferris and others in the matter. This committee discharged its duties. The result has been given above.

The new congregation took steps at once for the erection of a place of worship. By the first of May—within a month from the time of its organization—work had been begun on the present church edifice—and within a year, that is on the twenty-eighth of April, 1831, it is recorded that the Consistory met at the Church. Meanwhile the young church had been holding its services in the Academy, not the present brick building, but the older wooden part which now holds a humbler position in the rear.

The church was built,—as many churches were built fifty years and more ago—by a kind of speculation on the part of the builder. Some builder being assured of the sale of a part at least of the pews or slips in the church, took upon himself the cost of putting up the building, reckoning to be repaid by the sale of the pews.

These pews when sold became the property of the buyer and were subject to no assessment or tax for the payment of the expenses of the church or congregation. The owner might rent his pew to another and put the proceeds into his own purse. It is remembered that the speculation proved a disastrous one to the builder of this church, Mr. Ira Tillotson, the sale of the pews not making good the cost of the building.

Services were held for some little time in the basement of the church, while the upper audience room was being finished off. As finished at first, the audience room had its pulpit at the south end—the entrance end—and had galleries on the two sides and on the north end, at which end also was the place of the choir of singers. The galleries were taken out and the present form given to the audience room in 1860. In 1855 the private holding of pews was ended,—all the pews passing into the possession of the corporation. Up to this date,—1855—the salary of the minister had been raised by subscription—henceforth it was raised by the renting of the pews or slips.

In the early days of the church public services on Sunday were held both in the forenoon and in the afternoon, and there was a third service, of a less formal character, in the evening. This was changed in 1846, the afternoon sermon taking the place of the evening service. The question of the change had been discussed as early as 1832.

In August of 1830, Gen. Simeon DeWitt presented the young church with a lot of land. Gen. DeWitt was a large land-holder in the village. He had laid out streets, and had divided up his lands into lots and was now offering his lots for sale. The lot given the church corresponds nearly to the present number seventy of North Tioga street, and ran back to Sears Lane. The lot was soon sold, the money arising from its sale with other money was used in paying for the site of the present church edifice.

Richard Varick DeWitt also presented the church with the means of buying a communion service, which the Consistory voted should be of "the first-rate Sheffield plate."

In 1831, July 13, a "Sabbath School Society" was formed, and articles for its constitution and government adopted. It was to hold meetings on the second Monday of each month, the meeting on the second Monday of July being its annual meeting. It had its President always the Pastor,—its Vice-President, its Secretary, and its Treasurer, together with its managers, and somewhat numerous visiting committee, both male and female, whose duty it was to look up scholars for the school.

The teachers were to make monthly reports of the condition of their classes. The summing up of but one set of such reports is recorded that of September, 1832-—which gives an average attendance for five Sundays of sixty-eight scholars, the highest number being eighty.

The monthly meetings were kept up, with some irregularity, for a year or more, then only yearly meetings are recorded, till 1843, when with the election of its officers, the Society seems to have expired.

But not so the Sunday School of the church. That continued to exist, and has continued till the present time with members under Biblical instruction, sometimes greater, sometimes smaller, reporting at one time, 1867, its average attendance to be one hundred and fifty.

The first pastor of the church was the Rev. Alexander M. Mann, who began his labors in Ithaca, in June of 1830. On the eleventh of December of the same year, the Consistory gave him a "call to settle over us as our Pastor," at a salary of five hundred dollars a year, yet felt themselves under the necessity of asking the Missionary Society of the Dutch Church for help in making up this sum. There is no record of his installation, except, may be, in the records of the Classis of Cayuga.

Dr. Mann found the church a church of thirty-two members he left it a church of one hundred and forty-six members. No one of his successors in the pastoral care of this Church saw so many turn from the way of death to the way of life. During his pastorate one hundred and fourteen were added to the church by profession, and fifty-eight by letter The years 1831 and 1835 were years when men's thoughts were mightily drawn from the things of this world, to the things of that world to which all men are hastening

The records show no account of the sums raised by contribution in the church and congregation in the days of Dr. Mann, but it is remembered that the sums advanced by the Missionary Society of the Dutch Church in aid of the new organization were paid back, mainly by the labors of the women of the congregation.

Dr. Mann was born in Philadelphia in 1808. He was fitted for college at Somerville, New Jersey, entered the junior class of Rutgers College in 1825, and graduated in 1827. His theological studies were carried on and completed at the same place. His license to preach is dated 7th April, 1830. He arrived in Ithaca about the first of May of the same year. On the 27th of March, 1837, he resigns his pastorate because of "some peculiar considerations relating to himself." What these considerations were, they that are curious may possibly find explained in the catalogue of members.

Dr. Mann went from Ithaca to Troy, where he preached about a year; from Troy to the First R. D. Church in Poughkeepsie; thence in 1857 to Hoboken, N. J.; from Hoboken to Trumansburgh, in 1862. After three or four years in Trumansburgh, Dr. Mann removed to Farmer Village, where he is now residing in no regular pastoral work.

Dr. Mann was president of the General Synod in 1851. He received his degree of D. D., in 1853, from the University of Rochester.

Dr. Hoes, the second pastor of the church, was born at Middleburgh, in 1811, but was brought up at Kinderhook, and fitted for college in the academy there. He entered the Sophomore class of Amherst College in 1829, and graduated in 1832. His theological studies were pursued at Princeton, N. J., where he was licensed to preach in 1834. He became pastor of the R. D. Church in Chittenango in 1835, and of our church in 1837. After eight years' service here, he left upon a call to the R. D. Church of Kingston, where he preached till January, 1867. Since that date he has resided at Kingston, but in no regular pastoral work. His degree of D. D., came from Union College in 1852.

During his eight years' labor with us, one hundred and sixty-three were added to the church : fifty-four by confession, one hundred and nine by letter.

Dr. Hoes was followed by the Rev. James Vernor Henry. Mr. Henry was born in Albany in 1798. He prepared for college at Dr. Banks' Academy,—a school of some note in that day. He graduated at Princeton in 1815, entering Sophomore in 1812. After graduating he went to Edinburgh in Scotland, to the University there. He returned after two years' study and travel, and became tutor in his Alma Mater at Princeton. Here he served two years, and then took a full course in theology in the same place.

His first settlement as pastor was at St. Mary's, Florida, over the Presbyterian Church in that place ; next at Ballston Spa, in this state , then at Cold Spring ; then at Sing Sing, where he preached nine years, and where he buried his wife and three children.

Mr. Henry now resigned his charge and was abroad in Europe for a year. Upon his return he preached for a time in different places, but accepted no call to settle till 1846, when he became pastor of our church. His labors here ended in 1850, because of the " inadequacy of the salary for the support of his family, and because of not being able to get a suitable and commodious house in which to live."

This was his last pastorate, though he preached more or less till with in six months of his death, declining because of ill health several calls to settle. He died in Jersey City, where he resided the last nine years of his life, on the 14th of March, 1873. His second wife, Gertrude Mary, daughter of Edward Kerneys, of Scarborough-on-the-Hudson, still survives.

Twenty-eight members, sixteen by profession and twelve by letter, were added to the church during Mr. Henry's pastorate.

Charles H. A. Bulkley, the fourth pastor of the church, was born in Charleston, S. C., 22d Dec. 1818. He was graduated in 1839, at the New York University, and from the Union Theological Seminary in 1842.

After laboring in New Brunswick, N. J., in Janesville, Wisconsin, and Mount Morris, N. J., he was installed pastor of our church, 3 th April, 1851. His letter of resignation—apparently because of inadequate support,—is dated 15th Jan. 1853. From Ithaca, Mr. Bulkey went to Winsted, Conn., where he preached five years : thence to Patterson, N. J., which place he left to become chaplain to the first regiment of Gen. Sickles' Excelsior Brigade. After leaving the army he became pastor of the Congregational Church in Owego, and next of a church in Malone, where he preached five years. In 1876 he was settled at his present sphere of labor, at Port Henry in this State.

Thirty-three were added to the church by confession and eight by letter during Mr. Bulkley's labors.

In 1851, the church bought of Mr. Samuel P. Bishop, then of Cincinnati, a son of Daniel L. Bishop one of the founders and one of the first officers of the church, the residence of his deceased father on Geneva street, that it might serve as a parsonage or residence for the pastor of the chuch. It was sold in 1873, the congregation seemingly glad to be rid of the ever increasing tax for repairs, and the proceeds used in repairing the church building, and in paying for a new organ.

The Rev. Dr. Joachim Elmendorf was the Pastor of the church fifth in order. Dr. Elmendorf was born in Rochester in 1827. He fitted for college in Waterloo and Hyde Park. He graduated at Rutgers College, New Brunswick, N. J., in 1850. and studied Theology in the Divinity School of the same place.

His first settlement was in Ithaca in 1853. He resigns in July, 1855, the "only reason therefor, being his health, which requires relief from the labors and care of this pastoral charge."

He was next settled the same year. over the R. D. Church in Saugerties ; then in Syracuse in 1862 ; then in Albany in 1865, over the Second R. D. Church, and lastly in 1872, in Poughkeepsie, over the Second Church of the same name, where he is now pastor.

Dr. Elmendorf received his degree of D. D. from Union College, in 1865. He presided over the General Assembly of the R. D. Church in 1872.

Three by confession and two by letter were added to the church in Dr. Elmendorf's time.

The sixth pastor was the Rev. John W. Schenck. Mr. Schenck was born in December, 1825, at Cross Roads — now Dayton — in New Jersey. He is a graduate of Rutgers College, and pursued his studies in Divinity at the Seminary in the some place. His first plan was to give himself to missionary work, and had taken passage to China and put his goods on board of the vessel, ready for sailing. But Providence ordered otherwise.

He preached first at Tarrytown in the famous Sleepy Hollow Church: then at Chatham Four Corners : then in Brooklyn, N. Y., where he was instrumental in forming the present Bedford Avenue R. D. Church, then known as the East Church. From Brooklyn Mr. Schenck came to Ithaca in 1855. From Ithaca in 1863, was called to New Brunswick, N. J.; thence to the Third R. D. Church of Philadelphia ; thence to Pottsville, Penn to the First Presbyterian Church ; and thence to Claverack of this State where he is now settled.

By confession fifty-eight,—by letter twenty-seven were added to the Church during Mr. Schenck's eight years.

The Rev. Francis Zabriskie, D. D., the seventh pastor of our church, was born in New York city in 1832. He was educated at the University of the City of New York and at the Theological Seminary of the R. D. Church at New Brunswick, N. J. Before coming to Ithaca in 1863, he had been settled in New York City and in Coxsackie. He left Ithaca in 1866, upon a call to Claverack. He afterwards preached at Saybrook, Conn., and at Wallaston Heights, Mass., where he now resides.

In his three years' labor here, Dr. Zabriskie saw forty-nine added to the Church,—forty-one by confession, eight by letter.

The Rev. Dr. Strong, the eighth pastor of the Church was born in Flatbush, Long Island, May 23, 1824. He is a graduate of Union college in 1841, and of the Theological Seminary in New Brunswick in 1845.

He was ordained pastor over the R. D. Churches of Rosendale and Bloomingdale in 1845 ; settled at Newtown Long Island, 1849; over the R. D. Church on Bleecker street, New York city in 1859, and over our Church in May, 1866.

From Ithaca, Dr. Strong was called to Aurora in December, 1871, becoming pastor of the Presbyterian church in that place. In 1875, he took the Presidency of the Penn. Female College ; and in 1878 the Presidency of the Alleghany Collegiate Institute, and was installed pastor of the Central Presbyterian Church of Pittsburg the same year, which positions he now holds. At no time in its whole life had the church more members, and at no time were the yearly contributions so great as in the time of Dr. Strong.

Dr. Strong left in December of 1871, somewhat abruptly. During the first half of the year 1872, services in the church were held irregularly. A candidate or two appeared in the pulpit, but no action was taken. There seemed to be resting upon the minds of both church and congregation, the conviction that some change in the organization of the church and society must be made.

Sunday morning, June 30, notice was read from the pulpit, that there would be a meeting of the Consistory to-morrow morning at eight o'clock, and of the congregation at nine o'clock, "on important business.

The congregation accordingly met in the church and organized by choosing a chairman and a clerk. A resolution was now offered, that we invite the Rev. Mr. Dunham, who had preached the day before, to become the pastor of this church.

This resolution called forth much discussion. The point was made, and strongly insisted upon, that we must decide what we are to be, before we call a pastor—whether we are to remain in connection with the Reformed Dutch Church, or adopt some new organization and name.

The resolution was at length withdrawn, and another, which passed without dissenting voice, offered, namely : That it is expedient that the connection between this church and the Reformed Dutch Church cease.

A committee of three were appointed to draw up a petition to the Classis of Geneva, praying that this church be dismissed from its connection with said Classis. The committee was instructed to carry the petition to every family in the congregation. The committee obeying their orders, obtained some two hundred signatures to their paper..

Whatever difference of opinion, as to what change was necessary, may have existed before this meeting, there seemed after the meeting to be but one sentiment or purpose, among both church and people,—namely, to become Congregationalists. Every member of the Consistory, save two, joined in the movement. Men, who almost half a century before had had part in the forming of the church, and on whose shoulders for half a century the weight of the church had rested, not only assented to, but led the way in the change.

But an inclination to Congregationalism had long been a latent power among this people. Former pastors had seen this inclination, and had foretold that some day it would start into action. The day seemed to have come upon the departure of Dr. Strong. The University had brought several families of Congregational training into Ithaca. Some other families in the village were of the same sentiment. " It is useless," said one long an office-bearer in the church, and long one of its strongest supporters, "it is useless to dream of carrying on this church any longer as a Dutch Church."

The petition of the people thus numerously signed, was laid before the Classis at a meeting at Tyre. The Classis declined to receive it, on the ground that they knew only the Consistory, and could have no dealings with the congregation.

A petition to the same effect was forwarded to the Classis from the Consistory of the church, only two members dissenting. The Classis in their answer acknowledged the connection between the church and the Classis to be voluntary, but declined on their part to sever that connection.

Meanwhile the church and congregation went on in their plan and purpose. The church declared its connection with the Reformed Dutch

Church at an end, proclaimed itself an Independent Congregational Church, having first obtained from the courts authority for the change of name, and providentially, and most fortunately, obtaining the services of its present pastor, settled quietly down to its work.

But the Protestant Reformed Dutch Church of America, was not so easily shaken off. The Classis of Geneva sent down a committee to confer both with the Consistory and with the church. But neither the eloquence of Dr. Mann, the first pastor of the church, who was a member of the committee, and who pleaded most earnestly and warmly, that this church, a vine of his own planting—under God—depart not from the faith and the form at first taught them, and in which it had flourished almost half a century ; nor the weight and authority of the Classis made any impression. The church was steadfast in its purpose of changing.

With the Consistory the business of this committee was sheer ecclesiasticism. It did not seem commissioned to ascertain whether these things had fallen out to the furtherance of the Gospel, nor, like the apostle, to rejoice in that, from whatever motive, Christ was preached, nor did they seem, with the apostle, to know that there is a liberty wherein Christ has made us free,—but their business seemed to be, to fasten, if possible, the yoke of their ecclesiastical bondage upon an unwilling people, or, not succeeding in that, to keep in the possession of their denomination, property of no great value.

Failing in this, the next step was a resort to law. A complaint and petition—stretched out and elongated even up to twenty-thirdly, was laid before the Court, of which the gist—so far as one can see—was the asking the court to restore to its owners a certain piece of property which was even then in their possession.

The court dismissed the petition, but the case was carried up to the Court of Appeals. Technicalities being set aside, the question passed upon by the court is : whether a religious organization may rightfully change its name or denomination, there being no trusts. It may—was the decision of the Courts before which the case in succession came.

The language of the Court of Appeals—the court of last resort—is, "If property be given or granted to a religious society by words not plainly uniting the right to hold with the faith or doctrine of any particular denomination or body—the majority of the corporation control, and may use the property for any purpose which is religious."

Such is the conclusion of the "Ithaca Church Case," so far as legal rights and legal questions are concerned.

Gen. DeWitt must be allowed to know what he was doing, when in 1830, he made his donation to the young church. He knew that the new church was formed under the law of 1813, and that it possessed all the rights and powers conferred by that law ; and yet, with this knowledge plain before him, he made his donations.

In giving a village lot to the new R. P. D. Church of Ithaca, Gen. DeWitt did, by his deed of gift, no more unite the right to hold this property with the faith and form of worship of that denomination, than, when in 1826 he gave six lots to the "South Presbyterian Church in Ulysses," now Ithaca, or when in 1828, he gave a lot to the Baptist Church, or when in 1829, to the Episcopal Church in the village, did he connect the right to hold with the faith of any of these different denominations. He left them all to be guided by their own discretion in using his donations.

But what is Congregationalism ? First, let us ask what is a Church ? A church consists of, or is made up of, a number of persons who have associated, or united themselves together, for the purpose of professing and practicing the doctrines of the New Testament. Such an association is a Church of Christ. Such an association has, and can have, but one head, and that head is Christ. In such association, or such church, because of the infinite distance between the great Head of the Church and the individual members of that church, all the members thereof stand upon the same level, and are all equal before their great Head and risen Lord, no member having the smallest claim to any kind of authority over or among his fellow members. Such was the first Church of Christ on this earth—at Jerusalem—the names, about an hundred and twenty, over which not even the apostles themselves ventured to exercise the smallest authority, but on the other hand, submitted to the congregation—that is, to the assembled believers—the filling of the gap in their own number caused by the treachery of Judas Iscariot.

Such a church is, in its own sphere, sovereign and independent—it shapes its own creed and articles of faith ; it lays down its own rules of discipline ; it chooses its own officers, its pastors and deacons, but reminds such officers when chosen, that they are the servants, not the masters of the church.

Such a church is known among us as a *Congregational Church, because it vests all ecclesiastical power—under Christ—in the congregation, that is, in the assembled body of believers, or members of the
church.

It is here seen that a Congregational Church is a republic—a democracy—pure and simple, and as republicanism—or democracy—is the highest
and most perfect form of government among men, so Congregationalism
is the simplest, the highest and most perfect form or manner of manag-
ing matters ecclesiastic among men ; and the two are still further alike
in imposing great responsibility, the one, upon the individual voter,—
the other, upon each individual member of the church.

The number in this couutry of the so-called orthodox Congregational
Churches,—to which the name Congregational is commonly given—is
about three thousand.   But the great and influential Baptist denomination is purely congregational in its principles of church government, so
are the Christians, the Wesleyan Methodists, the Unitarians, and the
Universalists.   Indeed, of the whole number of churches in this coun-
try, somewhat more than one-half are, it is estimated, in matters of
church government, essentially congregational.

---

*The ancient churches of New England did not use to call themselves Congregational Churches :
while not refusing, they did not use the name. Among themselves they were simply Churches of
Christ ; and if more than one in the same town, they numbered themselves the first, the second,
etc., Church of Christ, in such town.

The Catalogue.

—

The catalogue contains the names of the members of the church for the years 1830–1879—it first half-century. It is drawn up in six columns—each column so headed as to show its use.

The names are arranged alphabetically under each date of entering, and then numbered from one to the last.

In the first column, the names of such as died while members are starred. In the fourth column, the date of death is given, also starred—and after the date, the age, in smaller figures. In a few cases the place of death—when not Ithaca—is found in the sixth column, starred. The other dates in the fourth column are dates of regular dismission from the church.

In the first column, a number in small figures is in some cases seen close after a name. This number refers to a father's or a mother's name.

The letters D, and E, after a name, show that such person bore the office of Deacon or Elder in the church.

Names in italics are the names of such as have become ministers of the Gospel.

The names of husband and wife, when both joined at the same time, stand the one directly after the other, when at different times, the name of the husband is found in the sixth column, as is also the case when the wife only, was, or is, a member of the church.

In the sixth column the letters s and r before a date, mean suspended or restored at such date.

The catalogue is by no means as complete as the committee, in whose hands the work was placed, could wish. But, whatever it may be, it is the result of much labor and pains. The column of names has only the completeness of the records, being a mere copy.

The attempt to find out what members died while members, and to find out the date of death, and the age, has cost many steps, nor is the labor repaid by the satisfaction of knowing that full information on these heads has been gathered in. It is feared that errors and omissions here exist.

In the third and fourth columns are many gaps. In the first pages of the catalogue, these gaps are caused by the fact that members of the church silently withdrew, mainly by removing from town, but asking for no letters of dismission. This cause of the gaps continues up to the latter pages of the catalogue. The number of members, therefore, absent and unaccounted for is great. But in the latter pages of the catalogue, these gaps are much increased, by the fact, that many names here are the names of members now resident in the village,—and increased further by the painful fact that a few names here are the names of some, who, having fallen from the faith which they once professed, and trampling under foot the covenant which they once took upon themselves, no longer worship and commune with us.

Of the thirty-two who formed the church in 1830, it is not known that any one is now living—the last survivor here among us in Ithaca, being the venerable Elder Johnson, of whom, as well as of two others, men prominent in forming the church, and in guiding the days of its infancy, the committee cannot close its labors without speaking.

Among the founders of the church no one is remembered with more affection than Elder Bishop. Quiet and gentlemanly in manner, he won the respect and attachment of all who became acquainted with him. He wore the Christian graces with such a charm, that others, who had little respect for religion, admired his consistent life. He was born in Lisbon, Conn. He came with his family to Ithaca at an early day in the history of our village, and engaged in merchandise. After a few years he closed up his mercantile business, and became connected with the old Cayuga and Susquehanna Railroad. He was an officer of the first Savings Bank of Ithaca, which after his death went into liquidation.

Having been called to Albany in the winter, to transact business for the Railroad, he was obliged to travel by stage from Auburn on his way home. The exposure, while he was laboring under indisposition brought on an attack of mortal sickness. Unable to reach home, he died suddenly at Ludlowville. The entire community, especially the members of the church he loved so well, mourned his loss as that of a friend and brother. The Consistory caused to be entered upon their records resolutions expressive of their deep sense of their loss, and of their sympathy with his family.

Augustus Sherrill is another name of weight and influence in the church in its first days. He was born in Richmond, Mass. He came to Ithaca and entered upon the practice of his profession—the law—early in life. Some years before the church was organized, his retiring manners and want of fluency in speech unfitted him for the duties of an advocate, but as a counsellor few men were his superiors. He held at different times several offices of trust and responsibility, the duties of which he discharged with admirable ability. In the church his counsels, when difficult questions were to be decided, were especially valuable. No one had more influence in the Consistory in all questions affecting the welfare of the church. He was quick to see the points of a question, and rapid in forming his conclusions. On such occasions his advice was given with much diffidence, and not with the air of a master. The Consistory, knowing his modesty and the soundness of his views, usually adopted his suggestions, and adopting, were seldom wrong.

With advancing years he yearned for the society and sympathy of his only daughter and her children, who were living in another part of the State. These longings at length constrained him to sever his connection with the church and the society in which he had spent so many years of activity and usefulness, and to remove to Piermont, N. Y., where he died. In the hearts of the older members of the church the name of Elder Sherrill lingers as a pleasant memory.

Mr. Abraham Johnson, the father of Arthur S. Johnson, came to Ithaca at the close of the last century, bringing with him his family, of which Arthur was one, and only five or six years old. After residing in the village—such as it then was—for a time, Mr. Johnson took up a farm, then all woods, about two miles and a half from the village on the present Danby road,—and here was passed Elder Johnson's youth. In the war of 1812, he volunteered, and served through the campaigns on our northern frontiers.

The war being over, he returned to Ithaca, and began the study of law, which profession he followed here in Ithaca, during a long and a useful life. He held various offices of honor and responsibility,—was Surrogate, Justice and Special Judge,—and of his decisions, it is said, none were reversed.

For forty-five years he held the office of Elder in the church which he helped found. He died at the advanced age of eighty-four years, leaving behind him the fragrance of a good name.

To the older members of the church—members whose memory runs back to the first years of the church—is the catalogue especially dedicated.   It will remind them of many a face now no longer seen among men, and of many a voice now heard only in the congregations of the church triumphant above.   It will remind them that the ties which draw them towards another world are growing more and more in number and in strength, while the ties which hold them down to this world are growing fewer and weaker.

Pastors.

1830,	-	- ALEX. M. MANN, -	1837, Mar. 27.
1837, June 21,	-	JOHN C. F. HOES,	- 1845, Oct. 3.
1846, Mar. 4,	-	*JAMES V. HENRY, -	1850, April 6.
1851. April 30.	-	CHAS. H. A. BULKLEY,	- 1853, Jan. 5.
1853, Nov. 2,	-	JOACHIM ELMENDORF,	- 1855, July.
1855, Oct. 22,	-	JOHN W. SCHENCK,	- 1863, Mar. 3.
1863. Oct 21.	-	FRANCIS S. ZABRISKIE,	- 1866, Mar. 13.
1866, May 27,	-	THOMAS C. STRONG,	- 1871, Dec.
1874, Nov. 18,	-	CHAS. M. TYLER.	-

Catalogue of Members.

NAMES.	IN, WHEN.	HOW, OR WHENCE.
1. *Daniel L. Bishop, E. - -	1830, April 2, -	Presbyterian Ch., Ithaca, -
2. *Mrs. Elizabeth Bishop, -	" "	" " " -
3. Elizabeth S. Bishop,¹ - -	" "	" " " -
4. *Mrs. Jane Cantine, - -	" "	" " " -
5. Isaac Carpenter, E, - -	" "	" " " -
6. John E. Cratsley, D. -	" "	" " " -
7. Mrs. Elizabeth Cratsley,	" "	" " " -
8. Joseph E. Cratsley, -	" "	" " " -
9. *Margaret Cratsley,⁶ - -	" "	" " " -
10. Isaac Day, - - -	" "	" " " -
11. *Mrs. Almira Gere, - -	" "	" " " -
12. Cornelius P. Heermans, -	" "	" " " -
13. *William S. Hoyt. D., E. -	" "	" " " -
14. Mrs. Lufanna Jaggar, -	" "	" " " -
15 *Arthur S. Johnson, E. - -	" "	" " " -
16. Levi Kirkham, D. - -	" "	" " " -
17. *Mrs. Huldah Kirkham, -	" "	" " "
18. *Cornelius Linderman, -	" "	" " " -
19. John C. Linderman, - -	" "	" " " -
20. *Mrs. Ann Linderman, -	" "	" " "
21. Charlotte Perkins, - -	" "	" " " -
22. Edward L. Porter. - -	" "	" " " -
23. Daniel Pratt, D.. E. - -	" "	" " " -
24. Mrs. Eunice Pratt, - -	" "	" " " -
25. Mrs Jane Rosencrantz, -	" "	" " " -
26. Philip C. Schuyler D, E.	" ".	" " " -
27. *Augustus Sherrill, E. - -	" "	" " " -
28. Mrs. Clarissa Sherrill,¹⁰² -	" "	" " " -
29. *Mrs Maria Stockholm, -	" "	P. R. D. Ch., Poughkeepsie,
30. Mrs. Harriet Tillotson, -	" "	Presbyterian Ch., Ithaca, -
31. *Mrs. Mary J. Woodcock, -	" "	" " " -
32. Henry Thos. Woodward, E.	" "	" " " -
33. *Mrs. Mary Dana, - -	1830, July 10,	Confession, - -
34. Richard McKinley. - -	" "	Presbyterian Ch., Ithaca, -
35. Mrs. Emeline Palmer, -	" "	" " "
36. *Mrs. Esther Vickery, - -	" "	" " " -
37. Mrs. Elizabeth Woodward,	" "	Cong. Ch., Hartford Ct.
38. *Mrs. Abigail Phillips. - -	1830, October 10,	Presbyterian Ch., Ithaca. -
39. Elizabeth Woodward,³² -	" "	Confession and Baptism,
40. Hester Woodward,³² - -	" "	" " -
41. Mary Bishop,¹ - - -	1830, December 5,	Confession, - -
42. *Adolphus Downer, - -	" "	" - - -

Out, When and How.	Whither.	Remarks.
1. *1848, Mar. 26, - 71	- - -	- -
2. *1856, June 20, - 73	- -	- - -
3. 1833, June, - -	- -	Mrs. Newton Perkins,
4. *1859, April 29, - 77	- -	Mrs. John Cantine,
5. 1838, June, -	Cong. Ch., Spencer,	- -
6. 1836, Nov. 4, -	Pres. Ch., Ludlowville, -	- - -
7. " " -	" " "	- - -
8. 1838, April 4, -	" " "	- - -
9. *1836, Oct. - -	- -	*Ludlowville, -
10. 1832, Aug. 30, -	Baptist Ch , Ithaca, -	- - -
11. *1831, Aug 19, - 4	- - -	Mrs. Luther Gere. -
12. 1832, May 6, - -	New York City, - -	M. D. - -
13. *1872, Nov. 1, - 6	- - -	- - -
14. 1831, May 27, -	- - -	- - -
15. *1875, Oct. 20, - 5	- - -	- - -
16. 1836, Aug. 31, -	Michigan, -	- - -
17. *1835, Aug., -	- -	- - -
18. *1848, Feb. 8, - 9	- - -	- - -
19. 1843, Sep. 18, -	- - -	s1842. r1843. -
20. *1841, Aug 3, - 5	- - -	Mrs. Cornelius L. - -
21. 1832, May 6, -	- - -	Mrs. C. P. Heermans.
22. 1862, Jan. 27. -	Westminster P. Ch., Detroit,	- - -
23. 1840, June 1, -	Pres. Ch., Marshall, Mich.	- - -
24. " " -	" " "	- - -
25.	- -	- -
26. 1847, Nov. 29, -	Cong. Ch., West Hill, -	- - -
27. *1853, Jan. 6, - 43	- - -	*Piermont. - -
28. 1853, Nov. 22, -	P. R. D. Ch., Piermont,	- - -
29. *1846, - -	- -	- - -
30. 1836, Aug. 31, -	- - -	Mrs. Ira Tillotson.
31. *1860, Sep. 27, - 76	- - -	Mrs. David Woodcock,
32. 1833, May 6, -	Ohio, - -	- - -
33. *1873, April 14, - 73	- - -	Mrs. Amasa Dana.
34. - -	Illinois, - - -	- - -
35. 1852, Jan. 30, -	Pres. Ch., Greenbush, -	- - -
36. *1831, May 19, - 27	- - -	- - -
37. 1846, Jan. 2, -	- - -	- - -
38. *1840, Jan. 21, -	- - -	- - -
39. 1833, May 6, -	Ohio, - -	- - -
40. " " -	" -	- -
41. 1847, Sep. 16, -	- - -	Mrs. James Thompson, -
42. *1841, Sep. 13, - 45	- - -	- - -

NAMES.	IN, WHEN.	HOW, OR WHENCE.
43. Mrs. Nancy Linderman, -	1830, December 5,	- -
44. William C. Phillips, -	" "	Presbyterian Ch., Homer,
45. Mrs. Almira Phillips - -	" "	" " "
46. Mary Phillips, - -	" "	" " "
47. Seymour Stevens, - -	" "	Confession and Baptism,
48. William B. Storms. -	" "	Confession,
49. Mrs. Cleantha Storms, -	" "	" - -
50. Isaac Winans, - -	" "	R. D. Ch., Bedminster, N J.
51. Stephen Winans, - -	" "	Confession, - -
52. Benjamin Woodward,[32] -	" "	Confession, -
53. Mrs. Loveday S. Woodward,	" "	" - -
54. Rosetta Adams, - -	1831, February 6,	Confession and Baptism, -
55. Mrs. Emeline Carpenter, -	" "	Confession. - -
56. Ann Maria Chatterton, -	" "	Confession and Baptism,
57. Cornelia Clark, - -	" "	" " "
58. Marcus Cratsley, - -	" "	" " "
59. Julia Cratsley,[6] - -	" "	" " "
60. *Warren B. Gay, - -	" "	" " "
61. Mrs. Susan T. Gay, - -	" "	" " "
62. *Mrs. Mary Grant, - -	" "	Pres. Ch., Geneva & Lansing
63. Amanda Hargin, - -	" "	Confession, - -
64. James M. Heggie, D. -	" "	Confession and Baptism, -
65. Daniel McKinley, - -	" "	Confession, - -
66. Mrs. Rachel McKinley, -	" "	" - -
67. Erasmus D. Moore, - -	" "	Confession and Baptism, -
68. Fanny Louisa Perry, -	" "	" " "
69. Emeline E. Phillips,[44] -	" "	Confession, - -
70. *Mrs. Rebecca H. Porter, -	" "	"
71. Mary Sherrill,[27] - -	" "	" -
72. James W. Taylor, - -	" "	Confession and Baptism.
73. John Tillotson, - -	" "	" " "
74. Calista Tillotson, - -	" "	Confession, - -
75. Catherine Vescelis, - -	" "	" -
76. *Mrs. Lorana Woodworth,	" "	"
77. Minerva Ballard, - -	1831, April 3,	" -
78. Mrs. Lucy Hayes. - -	" "	Cong. Ch., Hartford, Conn.
79. Mrs. Mary Ann Linn, -	" "	Presbyterian Ch., Ithaca,
80. Margaret McKinley,	" "	Confession, - -
81. Nancy McKinley, - -	" "	" -
82. *Mrs. Hannah Agar,	1831, May 1,	Presbyterian Ch., Ithaca,
83. Helen Carpenter,[5] -	1831, July 2,	Confession, -
84. Joanna Crane,[m] - -	" "	" - -

Out, When and How.	Whither.	Remarks.
43. 1843, Sep. 18,	- -	- -
44. 1831, Sep. 28 -	Utica. - -	- -
45. " " - -	" - -	- -
46. " " - -	" - -	- -
47. - - -	- -	- -
48. 1834, April 8 -	Bath. - -	- -
49. " " -	" - -	- -
50. - -	- -	- -
51. 1832, Mar. 20 -	-	- -
52. 1833, May 6, -	Ohio. - -	-
53. " "	" - -	- -
54. 1836, Jan, - -	- -	Mrs. Robert Ackland,
55. 1838, June,	Cong Ch., Spencer, -	Mrs. Isaac Carpenter.
56. 1836, Nov. 4, -	Presbyterian Ch,, Ithaca,	Mrs. Leonard Atwater.
57. 1851, Feby 25, -	" " "	Mrs. Wm. J. Totten.
58. - - -	-	
59. 1836, Nov. -	Ludlowville,	- -
60. *1870, Feb. 1, - 14	-	- -
61. - - -	- -	- -
62. *1841, Nov. 26, - 3*	- -	Mrs. C. L. Grant. -
63. 1833, May 6, -	Ohio, - -	Mrs. B. Woodward.
64. - - -	- - -	- -
65. 1836, June,	Caroline, -	- -
66. " " -	" - -	- -
67. 1831, April 10, -	Owego, -	- -
68. " Sept. 24,	Stockbridge Mass.	- -
69. " Sept. 28, -	Utica, - -	- -
70. *1837 June 8, - - 32	- - -	-
71. 1836, Aug 22, -	Deposit, -	Mrs. Hez. Seymour.
72. 1832, Mar. 25,	Owego, - -	- -
73. - - -	- - -	- -
74. 1837, Feb. 4,	- -	Mrs. William Bryan.
75. 1836, June 1, -	Presbyterian Ch., Ithaca,	- -
76. *1836, Dec. - - 2	- -	Mrs. Alvin Woodworth,
77. 1831, Nov.	- -	Mrs. Benj. Aldrich,
78. " " -	New York, - -	- -
79. 1834, Dec 4, -	Episcopal Ch., Ithaca,	- -
80. 1839, June 19, -	La Fox, Kane Co,, Ill., -	- -
81. " " -	" " "	- -
82. *1836, May 3, - -	- - -	*Mecklenburg.
83. 1838, June -	Spencer Cong. Ch., -	- -
84. 1836, Jan. 6, -	Newark N. J. -	

NAMES.	IN, WHEN.	HOW, OR WHENCE.
85. Mrs Jane Thompson, -	1831, July 2,	Confession, -
86. *Mrs. Roxanna Grant, -	1831, Septem'r 11,	Presbyterian Ch., Ithaca, -
87. Mrs. Lydia Perkins, -	" "	Confession, -
88. *Mrs. Annatie Schuyler, -	" "	Presbyterian Ch., Ithaca, -
89. Mrs. Cassandra Henning, -	1831, Novem'r 20,	Confession, -
90. *Mrs. Susan Hoyt, - -	" "	2d R. D. Ch., Albany, -
91. Simeon Middaugh, D. -	" "	Confession, -
92. Elijah H. Trowbridge, -	" "	Cong. Ch., Worcester, Mass.
93. Mrs. Elizabeth Trowbridge,	" "	" " '
94. *Mrs. Elizabeth Van Houten,	" "	R. D. Ch., Caroline, -
95. Mrs. Elizabeth Winans, -	" "	Confession, -
96. *George Blythe, - -	1832, January 22,	Presbyterian Ch., Ithaca, -
97. *Samuel J. Blythe. - -	1832, April 1,	' " "
98. Nancy Blythe, - -	" "	" " "
99. Benj. Durham, - -	" "	Confession and Baptism, -
100. Mrs. Hannah Middaugh,	" "	Presbyterian Ch., Ithaca, -
101. Mrs. Mary Olcott, - -	" "	Confession, -
102. *Mrs Mary Whiton. -	" "	Presbyterian Ch., Ithaca, -
103. Mrs. Elizabeth Bolton, -	1832, July 1,	Pres. Ch., Gratitude, N. J.
104. Jonathan B. Gosman, -	" "	Presbyterian Ch., Danby, -
105. Mrs. Jane Gosman, - -	" "	" " "
106. *Mrs. Harriet Quigg, -	" "	Presbyterian Ch., Ithaca, -
107. Mrs. Lucy M Schuyler, -	" "	Pres. Ch., Seneca Falls, -
108. *Mrs Mary Tourtellot, -	"	Confession and Baptism, -
109. Abram E. Miller, D. - -	1832, Septem'r 23.	Cong. Ch , Homer, -
110. Sarah Starkee, - -	" "	Confession, -
111. Mrs. -- Taber, - -	" "	" -
112. Edward Wood, - -	" "	" -
113. James Cooper, - -	1833, February 3,	" - -
114. Edward Cooper, - -	' "	Middle D. Ch., New York,
115. Mrs. Margaret Cooper, -	" "	" " "
116. John T. Emmons, -	" "	Confession, -
117. *Geo. E. Hand, - -	" "	Presbyterian Ch., Vernon,
118. *Peter P. Van Houten, -	" "	- - -
119. *Mrs. Ann Bogardus, - -	1833, April 1,	R. D. Ch., Warwarsing, -
120. *Mrs. Rachel Clark, -	" "	Confession and Baptism, -
121. Mrs. Eunice Wells Seaman,	" "	Cong. Ch., Colchester, Ct.
122. Sarah Wells, - -	" "	" " "
123. Mrs. Sarah Tufts, - -	" "	Confession and Baptism, -
124. Mrs. -- Borland, - -	1833, July,	Certificate, -
125. Mrs. -- Emmons, - -	" "	Confession, -
126. *Mrs. Sarah Jackson, -	" "	R. D. Ch., Shawangunk, -

Out, When and How	Whither.	Remarks.
85. 1842, Sept 27, -		
86. *1860, July 29, - ·²	- -	Mrs. Jesse Grant. -
87. 1836, Aug. 31,	Buffalo,	- -
88. *1851, Jan. - -	- -	Mrs. John H. Schuyler.
89. 1817, March 29, -	Lutheran Ch , Danville,	- - -
90. *1868, Feb. 10, - ·⁷	- - -	
91. - - -	- -	
92. 1849, April 16, -	P. Ch., Sheboygan F., Wis.	- -
93. " -	" " "	- -
94. *1842, Aug. 5, -	- -	
95. - - -	- -	
96. *1842, June 2, - · ³⁷	- -	- -
97. *1843, Feb. 2 , - ³²	- -	s. 1841. - -
98. 1836, June 1, -	- -	Mrs. Chas. Hadden.
99. 1834, Jan. - -	Ohio,	- - -
100. - - -	- -	Mrs. Simeon Middaugh.
101. 1833, Mar. 28, -	Lansing.	- - -
102. *1848, June 18, - ·³	- -	Mrs. John Whiton.
103. - - -	- -	- - -
104. 1836, Mar. 5, -	Danby,	- - -
105. - - -	"	- - -
106. *1863, Aug. 29, - ⁷²	- - -	Mrs. David Quigg.
107. 1847, Nov. 29, -	Cong. Ch , West Hill, -	Mrs. P. C. Schuyler.
108. *1875, Sept. 4, - ·⁴	- - -	Mrs. Jeremiah Tourtellot.
109. 1833, Sept - -	Delhi,	M. D. - -
110. - . - -	- -	- - -
111. 1838, March 2, -	- -	- - -
112. - - -	- -	- - -
113. 1844, April 13, -	- -	- - -
114. - - -	- -	- - -
115. - - -	- -	- - -
116. 1834, Apr. 14, -	Geneva. - -	- - -
117. *1841, - - -	- -	- - -
118. - - -	- -	s. 1844.
119. *1865, Nov. 12, -	- -	- - -
120. *1870, - -	- -	- - -
121. 1834, April 8, -	- -	- - -
122. " -	- -	- - -
123. 1836, Aug 22, -	St. Louis, Missouri, -	- - -
124. - - -	- -	- - -
125. 1834, April 14, -	Geneva. - -	Mrs. John T. Emmons.
126. *1837, April 13, ⁴⁰	- - -	- - -

NAMES.	IN, WHEN.	HOW, OR WHENCE.
127. Ann Pew, - - -	1833, July,	Presbyterian Ch., Owego, -
128. William Breese, - - -	1833, Septemb'r 1.	Confession and Baptism, -
129. Mrs. Esther Clark. - -	" "	" " "
130. Mary Mitchell, - . -	" "	" " "
131. James O. Towner, E. -	1833, Decem'r 15,	Presbyterian Ch., Peekskill,
132. *Mrs. Louisa Towner, - -	" "	" " "
133. Henry Krows, - -	1834, March 1, -	R. D. Ch., Warwarsing. -
134. Mrs. Ann Krows, - -	" "	" " "
135. Mary Taber, - - -	" "	Confession and Baptism, -
136. William H. L. Bogart, D. -	1834, April 13,	2d R. D. Ch., Albany, -
137. John J. Rezeau, - -	" "	R. D. Ch., Caroline, -
138. *Jacob Rezeau, - - -	" "	" " -
139. Mrs. Lydia Rezeau, -	" "	" " - -
140. Mrs. Nancy Tears, - -	" "	Presbyterian Ch., Dryden, -
141. Jeremiah J. Ayres, - -	1835, March 5,	Confession and Baptism, -
142. Mrs. Mary Barnard, - -	" "	Confession, - -
143. Samuel P. Bishop,¹ -	" "	" - -
144. Asa Bliven, - - -	" "	Confession and Baptism, -
145. Mrs. Janette Bliven, -	" "	" " "
146. Mrs. Abigail Bruyn, - -	" "	Confession, - -
147. Jane Bruyn,¹⁴⁶ - - -	" "	" - - -
148. Charles A. Buckley, - -	" "	Confession and Baptism, -
149. Almira Byington, - -	- - -	- - -
150. Vincent Conrad, D., E. -	1835, March 5,	Presbyterian Ch., Ithaca, -
151. Mrs. Diana Caroline Conrad,	" "	" " "
152. Sidney S. Cook, - -	" "	Confession and Baptism,
153. Mrs. Mahala Cook, -	" "	" " "
154. Caroline M. Cook, - -	" "	" " "
155. Jesse B. Cooper, - -	" "	" " "
156. Mrs. Content Cooper, -	" "	" " "
157. Mary Cratsley,⁶ - -	1835, March 8,	Confession, -
158. Sarah Deming, -	" "	Confession and Baptism, -
159. *James Dix, - - -	" "	" " "
160. Jacob Felthousen, - -	" "	Confession, -
161. Cornelius Henning, - -	" "	" - -
162. Elizabeth Henning, -	" "	" - -
163. Mrs. Mary McKinley, -	" "	R. D. Ch., Esopus, - -
164. Almira Middaugh,⁹¹ -	" "	Confession, -
165. Frederick Palmer, - -	" "	" - -
166. *Mrs. Elizabeth Partenheimer,	" "	Confession and Baptism,
167. Cornelia C. Partenheimer,¹⁰⁶	" "	" " "
168. Elizabeth Partenheimer,¹⁰⁶ .	" "	Confession. -

Out, When and How.	Whither.	Remarks.
127. 1834, Dec. 28, -	- - -	- -
128. 1836, Aug. 22, -	Vicksburg, - -	- -
1.9. 1858, Nov. 13, -	- - -	- -
130. 1834, Nov. 13, -	R. D. Ch., Catskill, -	- -
131. 1845, March 5, -	North Dutch Ch., Albany,	- -
132. *1841, Oct. 28, -	- - .'	- -
133. - - -	- - -	- -
134. - - -	- - -	- ..
135. 1838, March 2, -	Collins, - -	- -
136. - - -	- - -	- -
137. - - -	- - -	- -
138. *1844, May 11, -	- - -	s. 1841. -
139. 1844, Aug. 30, -	- - -	- -
140. - - -	- - -	- -
141. 1841, April 21, -	Pres. Ch. Williamsport,	- -
142. - - -	- - -	- -
143. 1839, June 19, -	Cincinnati, Ohio,	- -
144. - - -	- - -	- -
145. - - -	- - -	- -
146. 1877, - -	dis. by the classis, -	Mrs. Andrew Bruyn.
147. 1838, Aug. 18, -	Poughkeepsie, -	Mrs. A. M. Mann, -
148. - - -	- - -	s. 1836. -
149. - - -	- - -	- -
150. 1839, May 1, -	First R. D. Ch., Brooklyn,	- -
151. " -	" " "	- -
152. 1849, Sept. 15, -	- - -	- -
153. " -	- - -	- -
154 - - -	- - -	Mrs. Horatio S. Williams,
155. 1851, Sept. 5, -	- - -	- -
156. " -	- - -	- -
157. 1836, Nov. 4, -	Pres. Ch., Ludlowville,	- -
158. - - -	- - -	- -
159. *1843, Nov. 29, -	- - -	- -
160. - - -	- - -	- -
161. - - -	- - -	s. 1836. -
162. 1843, Jan. 9, -	- - -	- -
163. - - -	Illinois, - -	Mrs. R. McKinley, s. 1836
164. 1854, March, -	- - -	Mrs. Wm. Slocum, -
165. 1836, April 19, -	Pittsburgh, - -	- -
166. *1859, Oct. 28, - 72	- - -	Mrs. Adam Partenheimer.
167. 1842, July 1, -	Pres. Ch., Watsontown, Pa.	Mrs. David H. Watson.
168. - - -	- - -	- -

NAMES.	IN, WHEN.	HOW, OR WHENCE.
169. Margaret Partenheimer,[166]	1835, March 8	Confession,
170. James Pratt,	" "	"
171. Susan Pratt,[23]	" "	"
172. Emeline Quigg,[50*]	" "	"
173. Jane Schuyler,	" "	Confession and Baptism,
174. Mrs. Polly Smith,	" "	Presbyterian Ch., Ithaca,
175. *Albert A. Stannard,	" "	Confession,
176. *Catherine Stewart,	" "	"
177. *Sylvester Tillotson,	" "	"
178. Ellen Tourtellot,[304]	" "	"
179. *Mrs. Phebe Vickery,	" "	"
180. Augustus Whiton,	" "	"
181. *Lorana Woodworth,	" "	"
182. *Elizabeth Woodworth	" "	"
183. Jane Bogardus,	1835, May 3,	"
184. Enos Buckbee.	" "	Confession and Baptism,
185. Mrs. Eliza Buckbee,	" "	" "
186. *Henry Carpenter*,	" "	Confession,
187. John McKinley,	" "	"
188. Mrs Eliza McKinley,	" "	"
189. *Ellen Ann Monnell,	" "	"
190. Eliza C. Palmer,	" "	"
191. *Harriet Quigg,[50*]	" "	"
192. *Mrs. Elizabeth Stewart,	" "	"
193. *Jane Stewart,	" "	"
194. Marian Hawes,	1835, July 19,	"
195. Edmond H. Watkins, D., E.	" "	"
196. Mrs. Eunice Watkins,	" "	Confession and Baptism,
197. Mrs. Louisa Grant,	1836, January 3,	" " "
198. *Mary Linn,	" "	2d R. D. Ch., Albany,
199. Mrs. Amelia Mason,	" "	" " Utica,
200. Joseph Cooper,	1836, February 6	Presbyterian Ch., Pachogue,
201. Mrs. Esther Cooper,	" "	" " "
202. *Mary Mitchell,[130]	" "	R. D. Ch., Catskill,
203. Mrs. Mary Evans,	1836, May 1,	Presbyterian Ch., Ithaca,
204. Mrs. Mary Daniels,	1836, August 21,	Confession,
205. Mrs. Maria Terpenning,	" "	R. D. Ch., Esopus,
206. *Mrs. Hannah Holman,	1836, November 1,	Cong. Ch , Salem, Mass.
207. Sylvester Roper. D.	" "	Presbyterian Ch., Ithaca,
208. Mrs. Olive Roper,	" "	" " "
209. *Elizabeth Roper,	" "	" " "
210. James W. Taylor,	" "	Presbyterian Ch., Owego,

Out, When and How.	Whither.	Remarks.
169. - -	- - -	- - -
170. 1846, Dec. 4, -	Pres. Ch., Marshall, Mich,,	- - -
171. 1840, June 1, -	" " "	- - -
172. - -	- - -	- - -
173. 1851, May 30, -	Pres. Ch., Waverly, -	- - -
174. 1837, May 25, -	Bethel Ch., Troy, -	- - -
175. *1870, Dec. 28, - (2	- - -	s 1856. - -
176. *1837, Aug. 9, -	- - -	- - -
177. *1865, Dec. 14, - 44	- - -	*London, Canada. -
178. 1855, Mar. 26, -	San Francisco, -	Mrs. Chas. Stewart. -
179. *1835, Dec. 24, - 23	- - -	- - -
180. 1849, Sept. 20, -	- - -	- - -
181. *1871, Mar. 27, - 44	- - -	- - -
182. - -	- - -	*Auburn.
183. - - -	- - -	- - -
184. 1836, Nov. 23, -	Episcopal, Ch., Ithaca, -	- - -
185. " "	" " "	- - -
186. 1838, June, -	Cong. Ch., Spencer, -	- - -
187. - -	Illinois, - -	- - -
188. - - -	" "	- - -
189. *1871, July 17, - 53	- - -	Mrs. Albert A. Stannard.
190. 1859, Aug. 16, -	2d Pres. Ch., Nashville, Tn.	Mrs. Trenbath. -
191. *1870, July 3, - 51	- - -	- - -
192. *1857, June, -	- - -	- - -
193. *1847, Mar· 31, -	- - -	- - -
194. 1840, June 17, -	Pres. Ch., Danby, -	- - -
195. 1877. - -	dis. by Classis, -	- - -
196. " - -	" "	- - -
197· 1861, Feb 16, -	Dr. Springs Ch., N. Y. Cy.	Mrs. Wm. G. Grant. -
198. *1870, Jan. 29. - 85	- - -	- - -
199. 1839, June 19, -	- - -	- - -
200. 1841, Jan. 2, -	Pres. Ch., Mead Bank, -	- - -
201. " "	" " "	- - -
202. *1874, Jan. 19, - (2	- - -	Mrs. O. B. Curran. -
203. 1836, Aug, 31, -	Michigan, - -	Mrs. Levi Kirkham.
204. - - -	- - -	- - -
205. - - -	- - -	- - -
206. *1869, Oct. 20, -	- - -	- - -
207. 1858, Nov. 3, -	Pres. Ch., Danby, -	- - -
208 " "	" " "	- - -
209. *1860, Nov. 6, -	- - -	Mrs. Ebenezer Vickery.
210. 1839. June 19, -	Natchez, Miss. -	- - -

NAMES.	IN, WHEN.	HOW, OR WHENCE.
211. *Antoinette Strang, - -	1837, January 1,	Presbyterian Ch., N. York,
212. *Mrs. Margaret Bogart, -	1837, March 5,	2d R. D. Ch., Albany, -
213. Barbara Bogart, -	" "	" " "
214. Andrew Gillespie, - -	" "	R. D. Ch., Montgomery, -
215. Mrs. Elsie Gillespie, - -	" "	" " '
216. *Matthew Hoyt, D., E. -	1837, July 9,	Pres. Ch., Cherry Valley,
217. *Mrs. Mary Hoyt, - -	" "	" " "
218. Simon Schanck, - -	" "	R. D. Ch., Farmersville, -
219. Mrs. Julia Ann Schanck, -	" "	" " "
220. Mrs. Lucy M. Hoes, -	1837, Septem'r 3,	R. D. Ch., Chittenango, -
221. Geo. W. Nexsen, - -	" "	Coll. R.D.Ch., N. Y. City,
222. Mrs. Catherine M. Nexsen,	" "	" " "
223. John Dix, - - -	1837, Decem'r 20,	Cong. Ch., Richford -
224. Mrs. Sarah Dix, - -	" "	" " " -
225. Mary A. Dix, - -	" "	" " " . -
226. *Fidelia Dix, - - -	" "	" " "
227. Sophia Dix, - -	" "	" " " .
228. Jacob Rezeau, - -	1838, January 6,	Presbyterian Ch., Union, -
229. Mrs. Mary Ann Rezeau,	" "	" " "
230 Rebecca Schuyler, - -	" "	Presbyterian Ch., Ithaca, -
231. Margaret Blythe, - -	1838, May 5,	" " "
232. Marietta Blythe, - -	" "	" " " .
233. ' Susannah Blythe, - -	" "	" " "
234. William Huston, - -	" "	" " " -
235. Roxanna Huston, -	" "	" " " .
236. Henry Shields, - - -	" "	" " " .
237. *Mrs. Eliza Shields, -	" "	" " "
238. Geo. P. Frost, D., E. -	1838, July, 8,	" " "
239. *Mrs. Eliza L. Frost, -	" "	" " " .
240. Julia B. Frost, - -	" "	" " " . -
241. Mrs. Melissa Goddard, -	" "	Pres. Ch., Marlboro,
242. Albert M. Potter, - -	" "	" Dryden,
243. John H. Hawes, -	1838, Septem'r 2,	" Alden, -
244. Lewis Himrod, - -	" "	" Ithaca, -
245. Mrs. Harriet Himrod, -	" "	" " "
246. Henry Hammond, - -	1838, Novemb'r 3,	" " " -
247. Mary E. Bacon, - -	1839, March 3,	Confession, - -
248. Archibald Davidson, - -	" "	Presbyterian Ch., Ithaca, -
249. Mrs. Jane Davidson, -	" "	" " " .
250. Levi D. Ayres, - -	1839, April 21,	Presbyterian Ch., Romulus,
251. Mrs. Phebe S. Ayres, -	" "	R. D. Ch., Lodi, - -
252. Clara Berry, - -	" "	Confession and Baptism,

Out, When and How.	Whither.	Remarks.
211. *1841, Nov. 23, -	- - - -	- - -
212. *1839, Dec. 14, -	- - - -	- - -
213. 1850, Dec. 5,	- R. D. Ch., Geneva. -	- - -
214. 1846, Feb. 27, -	Pres. Ch., Sterling, Ill.,	- - -
215. " "	" " "	- - -
216. *1851, Dec. 21, -	- - - -	- - -
217. *1866, July 30, -	- - - -	- - -
218. 1845, July 29,	- R. D. Ch., Fairview, Ill.,	- - -
219. " "	" " "	- - -
220. 1845, Dec. 3,	- - - -	- - -
221. 1844, April 27,	- - - -	- - -
222. " "	- - - -	- - -
223. 1840, Oct. 30,	- Pres. Ch., Springport,	- - -
224. " "	" " "	- - -
225. 1838. -	Oregon, Missionary, -	Mrs. W. H. Gray.
226. *1838, Jan. 12,	- - - -	- - -
227. 1840, Feb. 1, -	Pres. Ch., Richford, -	Mrs. J. W. Robbins.
228. 1842, Jan. 9,	- - - -	- - -
229. " "	- - - -	- - -
230.	- - - -	- - -
231. - - -	- - -	Mrs. Anson Conrad. -
232.	- - -	- - -
233. - - -	- - -	Mrs. Patty. - -
234. 1845, April 21,	- R. D. Ch., Buffalo, -	- - -
235. " "	" " "	- - -
236. 1846, July 8,	- - - -	- - -
237. *1843, Dec. 18, -	- - - -	- - -
238. 1862, Oct. 22,	- Illinois, - -	- - -
239. *1860, Feb. 22, -	- - - -	- - -
240. 1853, May 2,	- Epis. Ch Ithaca, -	Mrs Henry Hammond.
241. 1850, May 6, -	20th St. Pres. Ch ,N.Y.Cy.	- - -
242. 1843, Mar. 29,	- - - -	- - -
243. - - -	- - -	- - -
244. 1840, May 2, -	Pres Ch., Elmira, -	- - -
245. " "	" " "	- - -
246. - - -	- - -	s. 1843. - -
247. 1840, Jan. 3, -	R. D. Ch. Utica, -	- - -
248. 1849, Dec. 17,	- Pres. Ch. Warsaw. -	- - -
249. " "	" " "	- - -
250. 1841, July,	- - - -	- - -
251. " "	- - -	- - -
252. 1842. Mar. 4, -	- - -	- - -

NAMES.	IN, WHEN.	HOW, OR WHENCE.
253. James Campbell, - -	1839, May 10,	Pres. Ch., New Hartford,
254. Camilla Dix, - -	" "	" Aurora, -
255. Mary Geddes, - -	" "	" Ithaca, -
256. John Besomer, - -	1839, July 5,	R. D. Ch., Warwarsing, -
257. Mrs. Nancy Scarborough, -	" "	Brick, Ch., New York City,
258. John Stevens, D., E. -	" "	Meth. Episcopal, Ithaca,
259. Mrs. Minerva J. Woodruff,	" "	Presbyterian Ch., Monticello
260. *Anson Conrad, D. - -	1839, November 1,	2d Presbyterian Ch., Genoa,
261. *Mrs. Margaretta Conrad,	" "	" " "
262. Mrs. Mary Ingersoll, -	" "	R. D. Ch., Lodi, - -
263. *Julia Young. - -	1839, Decem'r 21.	Confession, - -
264. Harriet N. Mitchell, -	" " 22,	Confession and Baptism, -
265. *Mrs. Priscilla H. Mitchell, -	1840, January 3,	R. D. Ch., Caroline,
266. *Mrs. Emma West, -	" "	Presbyterian Ch., Ithaca, -
267. Mrs. Mary Wood, - -	" "	" " " - -
268. *Mrs. Margaret Besomer,	1840, February 28.	Confession, - -
269. Mrs. Thankful Taber, - -	" "	Cong. Ch., Eden, -
270. Mary Taber, - - -	" "	" " " -
271. Mrs. Joanna Farnsworth, -	1840, May 2,	Congregational Ch., Danby,
272. *Jonathan B. Gosman, -	" "	" " "
273. Mrs. Jane Gosman, - -	" "	" " "
274. Eliza K. Gosman, - -	" "	" " "
275. *Abraham Gosman, - -	" "	" " "
276. Robert G. Kittle. - -	" "	" " "
277. Emeline Linderman, -	1840, July 2.	Presbyterian Ch., Fairport,
278. *Mrs. Mary Hanmer, -	" August 12.	Confession and Baptism, -
279. Mrs. Cordelia D. Ayres, -	" October 24,	" " "
280. Mary E. Bacon, -	1840, October 30,	R. D. Ch., Utica. -
281. *Mrs. Caroline Beers, -	" "	Congregational Ch., Danby,
282. John Freeland, - -	" "	2d Presbyter. Ch., Auburn,
283. Mrs. Phebe Freeland, -	" "	" " "
284. *Mrs. Wealthy Patterson, -	" "	Congregational Ch., Danby,
285. Mrs. Mary Ann Porter, -	" "	1st Cong. Ch., Hartford, Ct.
286 James Campbell, - -	1841, January 2,	Pres. Ch., New Hartford, -
287. Mrs. Sarah Monell, -	" "	West. Pres. Ch., N. York,
288. Augusta Monell, - -	" "	" " " -
289. Mrs. Mary Blythe, -	1841, March 14,	Confession and Baptism, -
290. Rachel Cain, - - -	" "	" " "
291. Edward G. Coy, - -	" "	" " "
292. *Mrs. Mahala Emory, - -	" "	" " "
293. Huldah A. B. Frost, -	" "	Confession, - -
294. Mrs. Caroline Roat, -	" "	R. D. Ch., Montgomery, -

Out, When and How.	Whither.	Remarks.
253. 1839, Sept. 28, -	1st Pres. Ch. Rochester,	- -
254. 1810, Oct. 30, -	Pres. Ch. Springport, -	- - -
255. 1810, May 2, -	Pres. Ch, mira, -	- - -
256. 1817, Aug 30, -	R. D. Ch , Caroline, -	- - -
257. 1843, Sept. 18, -	- - -	- - -
258. 1850, April 5, -	M. E. Church, Hillsdale,	M. D., -
259. - -	- -	- - -
260. *1852, May 14, - 42	- - -	- - -
261. *1816, April 19, - 34	- - -	- - -
262. 1810, Oct. 3, -	R. D. Ch., Lodi, -	- - -
263. *1877 Nov. 7, - 70	- - -	- - -
261. - -	- - -	- - -
265 *1855, Oct. 17, - 52	- - -	Mrs. John Mitchell. -
266. *1845, Aug. 21, -	- - -	- , -
267. 1875, Mar. 17, -	Pres. Ch., Cortland, -	• • •
268. *1845, April 29, -	- - -	- - -
269. 1852, May 29, -	Pres. Ch., Tonawanda, -	- - -
270. 1845, July 7, -	- - -	- - -
271. 1845, Mar. 5, -	- - -	Mrs. James O. Towner,
372. *1867, Jan. 31, - 70	- - -	- - -
273. - -	Albany, - -	• - -
274 1877. - -	dis. by classis. -	Mrs. Wm. Halsey, -
275. 1814, Mar. 18, -	- - -	- - -
276. 1847, Dec. 3, -	Cong. Ch. West Hill, -	- - -
277. 1819, Mar. 31 -	Pres. Ch. Elmira, -	- - -
278. *1840, Sept. 20, - 41	- - -	- - -
279. 1811, April 23, -	Pres. Ch., Williamsport,	Mrs. J. J. Ayres -
280. 1842, Mar. 4, -	- - -	- - -
281 *1871, Dec. 2, -	- - -	- - -
282. - -	- - -	- - -
283. - - -	- - -	- - -
281. *1866, Sept. 2, - 54	- - -	- - -
285. 1862, Jan. 27, -	Westm'str Pres Ch.,Detroit	Mrs. Edward L. Porter,
286. 1842. Jan. 9, -	- - -	- - -
387. 1844, Aug. 30, -	- - -	- - -
288. " "	- - -	- - -
289. 1848, Oct. 11, -	Varna, - -	Mrs. C. R. Weeks, -
290. 1844, Aug. 30, -	- - -	- - -
291.. 1843, Sept. 2, -	- - -	- - -
292 *1851, July 28, -	- - -	- - -
293. 1842, Sept. 27, -	- - -	Mrs. Chas. Fitch. -
294. - - -	- - -	Mrs. Andrew Teeter.

NAMES.	IN, WHEN.	HOW, OR WHENCE.
295. *Mrs. Emma Roat, -	1841, March 14,	R. D. Ch., Montgomery, -
296. Elvira Rosebrooks, - -	" "	Confession and Baptism, -
297. Mrs. Eliza Sutherland, -	1841, April 30,	Presbyterian Ch., Windham,
298. John W. Gott, - - -	" June 2,	R. D. Ch., Berea, - -
299. Sarah Jane Hogan, -	" August 25,	Confession and Baptism, -
300. Francis M. Sherrill,[443] -	" Sept. 5,	2d Pres. Ch., Troy.
301. Vincent Conrad, D., E. -	" Nov. 7, -	R. D. Ch., Six Mile Creek,
302. *Diana Caroline Conrad, -	" "	" " "
303. John M. Davidson, -	1842, January 2,	R. D. Ch., Lodi,
304. Caroline Davidson, - -	" "	" " - -
305. Isaac Linderman, -	" "	Presbyterian Ch., Fairport,
306. *Chas. F. Woodruff, D. -	" "	Confession and Baptism, -
307. Mrs. Mary Hanmer, -	1842, April 29,	Pres. Ch., Lewisburgh, -
308. Mrs Martha Jane Tilton, -	" "	" " Dover, -
309. *Mrs. Eliza Coryell, -	1842, July 1,	" " Ithaca, -
310. Joanna Crane,[105] - -	" "	4th Pres. Ch., Newark, -
311. Geo. A. Hart, - -	" 2,	Presbyterian Ch., Ithaca,
312. Mrs. Adeline E. Hart, -	" "	" " "
313. *Harriet Orne, - -	" "	Crombie St Ch. Salem, Mass.
314. Mrs Eliza Clark, - -	1842, Novem'r 6,	Confession and Baptism, -
315. *Mrs. Diana Coy, -	" "	Confession, - -
316. Margaret Ann Huston,[234] -	" "	" - - -
317. Geo. W. Schuyler, D, E.	" "	Presbyterian Ch., Ithaca,
318. Mrs. Matilda Schuyler, -	" "	" " "
319. Esther Elizabeth Jackson,	1843, January 1,	Confession, - -
320. Timothy Dwight Wilcox,D,E.	" "	2d Av. Pres. Ch., N. York,
321. Mrs. Margaret Ann Wilcox,	" "	" " "
322. Mrs, Mary Bennett, -	1843, March 3, -	R. D. Ch, Guilford, -
323. Angeline Bennett, - -	" "	" " "
324. David Davis, - -	" "	R. D. Ch., West Troy, -
325. *Julia E. Ackley,[418] -	1843, May 21, -	Confession, - -
326. Catherine E. Beers, -	" "	Confession and Baptism, -
327. David I. Chadwick, -	" "	" " "
328. Sophronia Chadwick, -	" "	Confession, - -
329. Nathan B. Cook, - -	" "	Confession and Baptism, -
330. Wm. H. Cunningham, -	" "	Confession, - -
331. Mrs. Mary Ann Freeman, -	" "	Confession and Baptism, -
332. Phebe E. Frost, - -	" "	Confession, - -
333. Letitia C. Hargin, -	" "	" - - -
334. *John C. Hayes, - -	" "	" - - -
335. Mrs. Miranda Hawley, -	" "	" - - -
336. *Mrs. Elizabeth Heggie, -	" "	" - - -

Out, When and How.	Whither.	Remarks.
295. *1858, Feb. 9, -	.	- -
296. 1851, - -	.	Mrs. Millspaugh. - -
297. 1844, Nov. 19, -	. .	- -
298. - -	. .	-
299. - - -	. .	-
300. 1841, Dec. 31. -	. .	Mrs. Gay. -
301. 1857, May 1, -	R. D. Ch , Chicago, .	- -
302. *1842, July 4, - ³¹	. .	. -
303. - -	. .	. -
304. - - -	. .	. -
305. - - -	. .	. -
306. *1849, May 26, - ³⁵	. .	. -
307. 1872, Mar. 11, -	Pres. Ch , Lewisburgh, Pa.	. -
308. - - -	. .	- -
309. *1871, Nov. 13, - ⁷¹	. .	s1852. - - -
310. - - -	. .	. .
311. 1847, Dec. 23, -	. .	. .
312. " "	. .	. .
313. - -	. .	. .
314. 1851, May 30, -	R. D. Ch., Syracuse, .	. .
315. *1856, Jan. -	. .	. .
316. 1845, April 21, -	R. D. Ch., Buffalo, .	. .
317. - - -	. .	. .
318. - - -	. .	. .
319. - - -	. .	. .
320. 1851, Feb. 26, -	Pres. Ch., Peekskill, .	. .
321. " "	" "	. .
322. - - -	. .	. .
323. - - -	. .	. .
324. 1847, Oct. 11, -	Pres. Ch., Saquoit, .	. .
325. *1846, Jan. 10, - ²⁵	. .	. .
326. 1853, Jan. 21, -	North R. D. Ch., Albany.	Mrs. W. U. Gregory.
327. - - -	. .	. .
328. - - -	. .	. .
329. 1844, Nov 4, -	. .	. .
330. - - -	. .	. .
331. 1851, May 19, -	Pres. Ch,, Trumansburgh.	. .
332. 1857, May 1, -	Pres. Ch., Horseheads.	Mrs. Boyd—Mrs. Breese.
333. - - -	. .	. .
334. *1858, Aug. -	,	. .
335. 1847, April 2, -	Episcopal Ch., Ithaca.	, .
336. - - -	. .	s1866. . .

NAMES.	IN, WHEN.	HOW, OR WHENCE.
337. Amanda G. Henning, -	1843, May 21, -	Confession, - -
338. Margaret H. Hinds, -	" "	" - -
339. Adelia Hoose, - -	" "	Confession and Baptism, -
340. Louisa F. Langstaff, -	" "	" " "
341. *Isaac T. Martin, - -	" "	Confession, - -
342. *Harriet Olive Martin, -	" "	" - - -
343. Sarah Jane Middaugh,⁹¹ -	" "	" - -
344. Mary E. Pratt, - -	" "	" - -
345. Mary Rezeau, -	" "	" - - -
346. James Thompson, -	" "	" - -
347. Frances M. Tourtellot,³⁹¹ -	" "	Confession and Baptism, -
348. Epaphras Warren, -	" "	Presbyterian Ch., Ithaca, -
349. Mrs. Belinda Warren, -	" "	" " " -
350. Mary Warren, - -	" "	" " " -
351. Nelson Boldsby, - -	1843, July 2,	Confession and Baptism, -
352. Mrs. Mary Boldsby, -	" "	Cong. Ch., Lisle
353. Clarissa Clark, - -	" "	Confession, - -
354. Elizabeth Clark, -	" "	Confession and Baptism, -
355. Harriet Ann Grant,⁵⁶ - -	" "	Confession, - -
356. William Halsey, D., -	" "	Confession and Baptism,
357. Joseph W. McKeen, -	" "	" " "
358. Mary Ann McKeen, -	" "	Confession, -
359. Eliza Jane Young, - -	" "	" - -
360. Isaac N. Beach, - -	1844, January 5,	Pres. Ch., Ballston Spa., -
361. Mrs. Elizabeth Beach, -	" "	" " "
362. *Mrs. Amy Halliday, -	" "	2d Av. Pres. Ch., N. York,
363. *Laura Hutchinson, - -	1844, May 3,	R. D. Ch., Caroline, -
364. Benj. Avery Atwater, D.,	" 5,	Confession and Baptism,
365. Mrs Sarah Ann Atwater, -	" "	" " "
366. Susan Davis,³²⁴ - -	1844, August 14,	Confession, - -
367. Catherine Davis,³²⁴ -	" "	" - -
368. Martha Davis, ³²⁴ - -	" "	" - -
369. Frederick Palmer, -	" " 30,	Cong. Ch., Sandisfield,
370. Camilla Dix,²²³ - -	" Nov. 10, -	Pres. Ch., Springport, -
371. Margaret Felthousen, -	1845, March 2,	Confession, - -
372. Esther Gay, - - -	" "	Presbyterian Ch., Ithaca, -
373. *Mrs. Sarah Butler, - -	1845, May 2,	" " "
374. *Mrs. Mary Conrad, -	" "	" " "
375. Mrs. Catherine McCormick,	" "	" " "
376. *Mrs. Mary Hargin, -	1845, July 5,	Congregational Ch., Genoa,
377. Calvin C. Godley, - -	1846, January 2.	Presbyterian Ch., Aurora,
378. Mrs. Martha Godley, ²²³ -	" "	" " "

Out, When and How.	Whither.	Remarks.
337. 1817, Mar. 29,	Lutheran Ch., Danville,	- - -
338. 1864, Feb. 5, -	R. D. Ch. Brooklyn, -	- - -
339. 1848, Nov. 27, -	Pres. Ch. Trumansburg,	Mrs. Bancroft. -
340. 1853, Feb. 26, -	Pres Ch., Elmira, -	s.1848r.1851 Mrs. JCCorwin
341. *1870, June 25, -	- - -	
342. *1869, Aug. 24, -	- - -	Mrs. Frank Atwater. -
343. 1857, Aug. 14, -	Cong. Ch. Owego, -	Mrs. Eli Drake. -
344. 1843, Sept. 18, -	- - -	- - -
345. 1844, Aug. 30,	- - -	- - -
346. 1847, Sept. 16, -	3d Pres. Ch., Pittsburgh, Pa	- - -
347. 1852, June 11, -	Meth.or Epis.Ch. Catherine	Mrs. Hazen, - -
348. 1856, Dec. 29, -	- - -	- - -
349. - -	- - -	s. 1856. - - -
350. 1849, April 13, -	Pres. Ch., Camden, N. J.	Mrs. John S. McCrea.
351. 1847, April 19, -	" Havanna,	- - -
352 " "	" " "	- - -
353. 1846, May 28, -	R. D. Ch., Albany, -	- - -
354. 1858, Nov. 13, -	- - -	Mrs J. C. Hayes,
355. 1850, Nov. 23, -	M. E. Ch., Ithaca, -	- - -
356. 1877. - -	dis. by classis.	- - -
357. - - -	- - -	- - -
358. - - -	- - -	- - -
359. - - -	- - -	- - -
360. 1849, Mar. 31, -	Cong. Ch., Provid'ce, R. I.	- - -
361. " "	" " "	- - -
362. *1849, Nov. 26, -	- - -	Mrs. Samuel Halliday.
363. *1864. -	- - -	Mrs. Hanford. -
364. - -	- - -	- - -
365. - - -	- - -	- - -
366. 1847, Oct. 15, -	Pres. Ch., Sauquoit. -	- - -
367. " "	" " "	- - -
368. " "	" " "	- - -
369. 1852, Jan. 30, -	Pres. Ch , Greenbush, -	- - -
370. 1852, Dec. 10, -	Pres. Ch., Clatsop I'ls. Or.	- - -
371. 1845, July 29, -	" Cayuga Bridge,	- - -
372. - -	- - -	Mrs Brace. - -
373. *1876, May 22, -	- - -	- - -
374. *1849, March 26, -	- - -	- - -
375. 1859, April 29, -	Pres. Ch., Port Jervis, -	- - -
376. *1853, Dec. 22, -	- - -	- - -
377. 1849, March, 14 -	Pres. Ch , Groton. -	- - -
378. - - -	" " "	- - -

Names.	In, When.	How, or Whence.
379. Francis L. Ackley,⁴⁵ -	1846, June 7,	Confession, - -
380. Catherine Andrus, -	" "	Confession and Baptism, -
381. Caroline Andrus, -	" "	" " "
382. Sarah Ann Blythe, -	" "	Confession, - -
383. Hannah M. Bruyn,¹⁴ -	" "	Confession and Baptism,
384. *Geo. M. Dana, - -	" "	" "
385. *Helen E. Dana, - -	" "	Confession, - -
386. *Harriet U. Drake, -	" "	Confession and Baptism, -
387. Henrietta A. Ferris, - -	" "	Confession, - -
388. Margaret A. Hance, -	" "	Confession and Baptism, -
389. Mrs. Gertrude M. Henry,	" "	Presbyterian Ch., Sing Sing,
390. Francis R. Johnson,¹⁵ -	" "	Confession, - -
391. *Sarah F. McCormick, -	" "	" - -
392. Mary L. Peters, - -	" "	" - -
393. Clarissa Roper,²⁰⁷ -	" "	" - -
394. *Jeremiah Tourtellot, -	" "	Confession and Baptism, -
395. Charlotte C. Beers, - -	1846, August 2.	" " "
396. *Mary Linn DeWitt, -	" "	Confession, - -
397. *Alvin Woodworth, - -	" "	" - -
398. *Horace King, - -	1847, July, 2,	Confession and Baptism, -
399. Mrs. Eliza Hance, - -	1848, February 4,	Pres. Ch., Cape Vincent, -
400. Stephen M. Culver, -	1848, March 29,	Confession, - -
401. James R. Henry, - -	" "	" - -
402. Mary E. Sheppard, -	" "	Confession and Baptism, -
403. *William Bryan, D., -	" " 31,	Confession. - -
404. *Elizabeth Middaugh,⁹¹ -	" "	" - -
405. Josephine Sherrill,⁴⁸ -	" "	" -
406. Daniel E. Bishop,¹ -	1848, July 1,	" - -
407. Mrs. Eliza L. Bishop, -	" "	" - - -
408. Edward J. Morgan, -	" Sept. 1,	" - - -
409. *Frances Conrad, - -	1849, June 28,	Presbyterian Ch., Ithaca, -
410. *S. Lewis Sibley, D., E. -	" "	Cong. Ch , Cutchogue, L. I.
411. *Mary A. Dana, - -	" August 31,	Pres. Ch., Niles, Mich.,
412. Mrs. F. Selover, - -	" "	R.D.Ch., Market St , N. Y.
413. Catherine Kincaid, - -	1850, January 29,	R. D. Ch., Berea, - -
414. James W. Taylor, -	" "	Presbyterian Ch., Owego,
415. Mrs. Susan H. Taylor, -	" "	" " " -
416. Eliza Seeley, - -	1850, April 5,	Congregational Ch., Danby,
417. Elizabeth D. Thompson,	1851, January 31,	Broadway Tabernacle Ch ,
418. *Mrs. Lydia Ackley, -	1851, April 6,	Confession, - -
419. Frederick K. Andrus, D., -	" " .	Confession and Baptism, -
420. Eliza P. Andrus, -	" "	" " " . -

Out, When and How	Whither.	Remarks.
379. - - -	- - -	- - -
380. 1850, Nov. 9, -	Pres. Ch., Bath, -	Mrs. Edwin F. Church,
381. 1853, Feb 26, -	Pres. Ch., Elmira, -	Mrs. Nathan G. Herrick.
382. 1856, Feb. 27, -	" Woodstock, Ill.,	Mrs Hewitt. -
383. 1872, Dec. 7, -	" Ithaca, -	Mrs. Byron Dana. -
384. *1850. - - 19	- - -	- - -
385. *1849, April 28, 17	- - -	- - -
386. - - -	- - -	Mrs. Geo. C. Hall,
387. 1853, Feb. 26, -	Pres. Ch., Elmira, -	- - -
388. 1857, July 25, -	" Bloomington, Ill.	Mrs. Furzeman. -
389. 1855, Sept. 17. -	- - -	- - -
390. 1850, Nov. 23, -	Meth. Ch., Ithaca, -	Mrs Chamberlain.
391. *1855, Dec. 30, - -	- - -	Mrs. Wm. V. Bruyn. -
392. 1875, Nov. 5, -	Aurora st.,M. E. Ch. Ithaca	Mrs. Dr. Coryell.
393. 1858, Nov. 3, -	Prs. Ch., Danby, -	- - -
394. *1853, July 20, - 7.	- - -	- - -
395. - - -	- - -	Mrs. Jonas B. Conkling.
396. *1871, Mar. 20, - 52	- - -	- - -
397. *1851, Feb. 12. - 72	- - -	- - -
398. *1847, Dec. 22, - 53	- - -	- - -
399. 1854, April 10,	Pres. Ch., Bloomington, Ill	- - -
400. - - -	California. - -	- - -
401. 1855, Sept. 17, -	- - -	- - -
402. - - -	- - -	Mrs. J. B. Terry.
403. *1867, Dec. 7, - 71	- - -	- - -
404. 1850. Nov. 6, - 25	- - -	- - -
405. 1848, Dec. 11, -	Epis. Ch., Waterloo. -	- - -
406. 1856, Aug. 1, -	- - -	- - -
407. " "	- - -	- - -
408. - - -	- - -	M. D. - -
409. *1878, July 4, - 7	- - -	- - -
410. *1864, April 25, 43	- - -	M D. - -
411. - - -	- - -	Mrs. S. M. Culver, *Cal.
412. 1861, Sept. 30, -	1st Pres. Ch., Hornellsville.	- - -
413. 1867, March 18, -	- - -	Mrs. Stephen Ferris.
414. 1854. Nov. 10, -	Pres. Ch., Gowanda, -	- - -
415. " "	" "	- - -
416. - - -	- - -	- - -
417. - - -	- - -	- - -
418. *1871, Mar. 23, 77	- - -	- - -
419. - - -	- - -	- - -
420. 1858, Jan. 1, -	- - -	Mrs. John Murdock.

NAMES.	IN, WHEN.	HOW, OR WHENCE.
421. Lydia J Barnum,	1851, April 6,	Confession and Baptism, -
422. Clarissa T. Bryan,⁴ -	" "	Confession, - -
423. Harriet E Bryan,⁴ᶜ -	" "	" - -
424. Mrs. Jane Cole, - -	" "	" - -
425. Jacob G. Conrad, -	" "	Confession and Baptism, -
426. Mrs. Elizabeth Conrad, -	" "	" " "
427. Mrs. Catherine A. Conrad,	" "	Cong. Ch. Stratford, -
428. Mrs. Mary E. Conrad, -	" "	Confession and Baptism, -
429 Mary E. Gay,⁴⁰ -	" "	Confession, - -
430. Calvin C. Godley, - -	" "	Congregational Ch., Groton
431. Mrs. Martha Godley,²⁴ -	" "	" " "
432. William G. Grant, D., -	" "	Confession, - -
433. Mrs. Harriet Grant, -	" "	Confession and Baptism, -
434. Sylvanus B. Hance, -	" "	" " "
435. Susan G. Hollingsworth,	" "	Confession, -
436. *Mrs. Charlotte G. Johnson,⁴⁶	" "	Confession and Baptism, -
437. *Mary J. Johnson,¹⁵ -	" "	Confession, - -
438. Eunice A. Martin, - -	" "	" - -
439. Helen Quigg,⁵ˣ -	" "	" - -
440. Susan M. Schuyler,²⁰ -	" "	" - -
441. *Mary E. Seely, -	" "	"
442. Harriet E. Shepard, -	" "	Confession and Baptism,
443. Henry W. Sherrill, -	" "	Confession, - -
444 Augustus C. Taylor, -	" "	" - -
445. Elias Tillotson, - -	" "	" - -
446. Mary G. Tillotson, -	" "	" - -
447. Eliza Van Hoesen, -	" "	Confession and Baptism, -
448. Mrs. Caroline A. Winton,¹⁵	" "	Confession, - -
449. Mrs. Almira S. Livermore,	1851, May 30,	Cong. Ch., Richford, -
450. *Mrs. Lucy M. Schuyler,²⁴ -	" "	" West Hill, -
451. Amos. T. Ward, -	" "	Confession, - -
452. Mrs. Anna M. Bulkley,	1851, August 2,	Presbyterian Ch., Mt. Morris,
453. *Mary Daniels, -	" "	Confession, - -
454. Mrs. Amanda S. Pomeroy,	" "	Pres. Ch., Seneca Falls, -
455. *Mrs Jane A. Ridgeway,	1852, June 13,	R. D. Ch., Caroline, -
456. Solomon Steckel, -	" July 30,	South R. D. Ch , N. York,
457. Mrs. Emeline Steckel,	" "	" " "
458. Gertrude Hageman,	" October 1,	Pres. Ch., Trenton, N. J. -
459. Mrs. Nancy Hammond,	1853, Septem'r 30,	" " Havana, -
460. *Mrs· Hannah Hoose,	" December 2	Confession and Baptism, -
461. *Philip Foote, -	1854, June 2,	Confession, - -
462. Mrs. Sarah Elmendorf,	1855, February 2	Pres. Ch., Seneca Falls, -

Out, When and How.	Whither.	Remarks.
421. - - -	- - -	- - -
422. 1855, April 16, -	Pres Ch., Great Bend.	Mrs. Simpson.
423. 1861, May 25, -	Cong. Ch., Danby, -	Mrs. T. H. Howell. -
424. 1852, July 3, -	Pres. Ch., Burdett, -	- - -
425. 1851, Dec. 5, -	M. E. Ch., Ithaca, -	- - -
426 " " -	" " "	- - -
427. 1857, May 1, -	R. D. Ch., Chicago, -	- - -
428. 1856, Oct. 17, -	- - -	- - -
429. - - -	- - -	Mrs. H. J. Smith, -
430. 1853. Mar. 21, -	Pres. Ch., Clatsop Pls , Or.	- - -
431. " "	" " "	- - -
432. 1861, Feb. 16, -	Brick Ch. New York, -	- - -
433. - - -	- - -	Mrs. Henry J. Grant,
434. 1854, April 10, -	Pres. Ch., Bloomington, Ill.	- - -
435. 1854, Sept. 25, -	Pres. Ch., Irvington., -	- - -
436. *1880, Jan. 11, - 70	- - -	Mrs. Arthur S. Johnson.
437. *1862, Dec. 10, -	- - -	- - -
438. 1865, Dec. 16, -	Cong. Ch., Rippon, Wis.	- - -
439. - - -	- - -	Mrs. Jefferson Beardsley.
440. - - -	- - -	Mrs. M. Lyon. -
441. *1852, Jan. -	- - -	- - -
442. - - -	- - -	- - -
443. - - -	- - -	- - -
444. 1854, April 10, -	Pres. Ch., Bloomington, Ill.	- - -
445. - - -	- - -	- - -
446. - -	- - -	Mrs. F. K. Andrus, -
447. 1854, Sept. 25, -	- - -	Mrs. E. Mallory. -
448. - - -	- - -	Mrs Samuel H. Winton.
449. - - -	- - -	Mrs Obadiah Livermore.
450. *1855, Sept. 20, 48	- - -	- - -
451. 1856, June 2, -	R. D. Ch., Kalamazoo, Mch	- - -
452 1854, Nov. 27, -	- - -	- - -
453. *1877, May 4, - 43	- - -	- - -
454. 1862, Mar. 18, -	Westminster Pres. Ch., Utica	- - -
455. *1870, June 27, - 65	- - -	Mrs. James Ridgway.
456. - -	- - -	- - -
457. - -	- - -	- - -
458. 1856, March 31, -	Pres. Ch., Milwaukee, -	- - -
459. 1861, May 21, -	Springfield, Ill. -	- - -
460. *1867, May 19, - 71	- - -	- - -
461. *1858, Aug. -	- - -	- - -
462. 1855, Dec. 24, -	R. D. Ch., Saugerties, -	- - -

NAMES.	IN, WHEN.	HOW, OR WHENCE.
463. *Cornelins Conover,	1855, August 3;	Confession,
464. Mrs. Sarah Garrett,	" November 2,	"
465. Mrs. Elvira A. Millspaugh,	" "	Letter returned,
466. Mrs. Sophia L. Schenck,	" "	R. D. Ch., Brooklyn,
467. Eliza Van Hoesen,	" "	Letter returned,
468. Harriet M. Rosebrook,	1856, August 1,	Pres. Ch., Sturgis, Mich.
469. Mary C. Woodruff,306	" "	Confession,
470. *Apollos Eaton, D.,	" October 31,	Presbyterian Ch., Varna,
471. *Mrs. Maria Eaton,	" "	" " "
472. Emeline Eaton,470	" "	" " "
473. Adaline Eaton,470	" "	" " "
474. Minerva Brownell,	1857, January 30,	Meth. Ch , Ithaca,
475. Timothy D. Wilcox, D., E.	" February 20,	1st Pres. Ch , Peekskill,
476. Mrs. Margaret A. Wilcox,	" "	" " "
477. Martha Schuyler,317	" May 1,	Confession,
478. Sarah E. Atwater 344	1857, August 2,	"
479. Martin F. Elmendorf,	" "	"
480. Henry J Grant, Jr.	" "	Confession and Baptism,
481. Elizabeth Iredell,	" "	" " "
482. Emma C. McCormick,	" "	Confession,
483. Lucy M. Schuyler,26	" "	"
484. William F. Smith,	" "	"
485. *Mary Troupe,	" "	"
486. Mrs. Mary Everett.	1858, February 5,	West. Pres. Ch., N. York,
487. John Justus Glenzer, D.,	" "	Confession,
488. Jennie Goodfellow.	" "	"
489. Sarah M. Livermore,502	" "	"
490. Samuel H. Wilcox,320	" "	"
491. Mrs Susan E. Atwater,	1858, April 30,	"
492. *James H. Conrad,	" "	"
493. Thomas F. Crane,	" "	"
494. *Theron Davenport,	" "	Confession and Baptism,
495 Mrs. Lucy Davenport,	" "	" " "
496. George Dixon,	" "	Confession,
497. Mrs. Helen Dixon,	" "	"
498. Maria L. Eaton,470	" "	"
499. Fanny M. Garrett,	" "	Confession and Baptism,
500. *Charlotte Heggie,4	" "	Confession,
501. *Mrs. Orrill Ann Hurd,	" "	Confession and Baptism,
502. *Obadiah L. Livermore,	" "	" " "
503. Lucy M. Middaugh,4	" "	Confession,
504. *Adnah Neyhart,	" "	Confession and Baptism,

Out, When and How.	Whither.	Remarks.
463. *1858, Feb. 4, - ·	- - -	- - -
464. - -	- - -	- - -
465. - -	- - -	- - -
566. 1863, Nov. -	- - -	- - -
467. - -	- - -	Mrs. E. Mallory.
468. 1860, May 4, -	R. D. Ch.,Constantine,Mch	- - -
469. 1871, May 1, -	Epis. Ch., Ithaca.	Mrs. Leander King.
470. *1859, Dec. 29, - 5(	- - -	- - -
471. *1862, Nov. 2, - 57	- - -	- - -
472. - -	- - -	- - -
473. - -	- - -	- - -
474. - -	- - -	- - -
475. - -	- - -	- - -
476. - -	- - -	- - -
477. 1871, May 1, -	Epis. Ch., Ithaca.	Mrs. C. L. Grant, jr.
478. 1863, Dec. 8, -	Pres Ch., Fairfield, Minn.	Mrs. D. A. Williams.
479. 1858, Jan. 19, -	- - -	- - -
480. - -	- - -	- - -
481. - -	- - -	- - -
482. 1859, April 29, -	Pres. Ch., Port Jervis.	Mrs. B. C. Farnum.
483. - -	Cong. Ch., Topeka, Kan.	Mrs Sheldon.
484. - -	- - -	- - -
485. *1868, Feb 9, -	- - -	Mrs. Van Rensalaer.
486. 1866, Jan. 3. -	Pres. Ch., Ithaca.	- - -
487. - -	- - -	- - . -
488. - -	' - -	- - -
489. - -	- - -	Mrs. Austin N. Hungerford.
490. - -	- - -	- - -
491. - -	- - -	Mrs. Edward Atwater.
492. *1865, Nov. -	- - -	- - -
493. 1859, April 14, -	1st Pres., Ch., Elizb'tn N.J.	- - -
494. *1871, March 16, 50	- - -	- - -
495. 1877, May 12, -	dis. by classis.	- - -
496. - -	- - -	- - -
497. - -	- - -	- - -
498. - -	- - -	- - -
499. - -	- - -	- - -
500. *1864. June 15, - 22	- - -	- - -
501. 1872, June, 14 - 51	- - -	- - -
502. *1858, May 22, - 62	- - -	- - -
503. 1870, Dec. 29, -	- - -	Mrs. John Degraw. -
504. - -	- - -	- - -

NAMES.	IN, WHEN.	HOW, OR WHENCE.
505. Jerome Norton, - -	1858. April 30,	Confession and Baptism, -
506. Mrs. Louisa Norton, .	" "	" " "
507. Harrietta E. Parker, .	" "	" " "
508. *David Quigg. - -	" "	Confession, - -
509. Mrs. Julia A. Quigg, .	" "	" - -
510. Elizabeth Rasbach, -	" "	" - -
511. Moses Reeves, - -	" "	Confession and Baptism, -
512. *John F. Shaw,*529* -	" "	" " "
513. James H. Smith, - -	" "	" " "
514. Mrs. Mary J. Smith, -	" "	" " "
515. Jonathan Snyder. - -	" "	R. D. Ch., Kingston, -
516. Mrs. Maria H. Snyder, -	" "	" " "
517. Mary K. Stout, - -	" "	Confession and Baptism, -
518. Helen M. Wilcox.321 -	" "	Confession, - .
519. Mrs. Mary E. Williams, -	" "	Confession and Baptism, -
520. *Daniel T. Wood, E. -	" "	Confession, - .
521. *Mary A. Woodney, -	" "	Confession and Baptism, -
522. Charlotte E. Mitchell, -	1858, July 30,	" " ",
523. Geo. Rankin, D. - .	" "	University Pl. Pres.Ch.N.Y.
524. Mrs. Mary Rankin,486 -	" "	" " "
525. Julia M. Shaw,529 - -	" "	Confession and Baptism, -
526. Sarah P. T. Beebe, .	" Novem'er 5,	N.W. R. D. Ch , N. York,
527. Mrs. Julia A. Atwater, -	1859, February 4	Confession and Baptism, -
528. Mrs, Mary F. Ridgeway,	" "	Meth. Ch.. Canoga, -
529. Anning O. Shaw, - -	" "	1st Meth. Ch., Ithaca, -
530. Adeline Eldred, -	" April 29,	Confession, - -
531. Evelyn Schuyler,317 .	" "	" - -
532. *Mrs. Amelia M. Eaton, -	" August 5,	" - -
533. Louise M. Woodruff,366 -	" "	" - -
534. Mrs. Eliza Dunham, -	1860, February 3,	" - -
535. Mrs. Jane Ann Fowler, -	" "	R. D. Ch., Farmerville, -
536. Mrs. Pamelia Patterson,	" "	Cong. Ch., Virgil, -
537. Samuel D. Sawyer, D. -	" "	R. D. Ch., Athens, Penn. -
538. Harriet W. Thompson, -	" Novem'er 2,	R. D. Ch., Bergen, N. J.
539. Helen M. Thompson, -	1861, February 3,	Confession and Baptism, -
540. Susan Settle, - -	" May 3,	R. D. Ch., Manheim, Ger.,
541. Mrs. Mary Smith, - -	" "	Confession and Baptism, -
542. *Mrs. Angelica Weidman,	" "	R. D. Ch.. Manheim, Ger.,
543. Mrs. Mary A. Freeman, -	" August 13,	Pres. Ch., Trumansburg, -
544. Marcus Lyon, D., E. -	" November 1,	Confession, -
545. *Mrs. Helen Aldrich, - -	1862, January 31,	" - -
546. Louise C. Johnson,15 .	" May 2,	" - -

Out, When and How.	Whither.	Remarks.
505. - - -	- - -	- - -
506. 1877. - -	dis. by classis.	- - -
507. - - -	- - -	- - -
508. *1862, Dec. 17, - ⁻²	- - -	- - -
509. - - -	- - -	Mrs. James Quigg.
510. - - -	- - -	Mrs David Townley.
511. - - -	- - -	- - -
512. - - -	- - -	- - -
513. - - -	- - -	- - -
514. - - -	- - -	- - -
515. 1861, Sept. 27, -	2d R. D. Ch., Kingston,	- - -
516. " "	" " "	- - -
517. - - -	- - -	- - -
518. - - -	- - -	Mrs. Dudley F. Finch.
519. - - -	- - -	Mrs. John A. Williams.
520. *1873, June 6, - ⁷³	- - -	- - -
521. *1859, Sept. 22, -	- - -	Mrs. L. Yates. -
522. - - -	- - -	- - -
523. 1866, Jan. 3, -	Presbyterian Ch., Ithaca, -	- - -
524. " "	" " "	- - -
525. - - -	- - -	- - -
526. 1869, Mar. 3, -	Westminster Pres. Ch.,Utica	- - -
527. - - -	- - -	Mrs Stephen D. Atwater.
528. - - -	- - -	Mrs. Fred. A. B. Ridgway.
529. - - -	- - -	- - -
530. 1874, May 20 - -	Pres. Ch., Dryden,	Mrs. Albert N. Prentsss.
531. - - -	- - -	Mrs. Chas. A. Schaeffer.
532. *1862, Feb. 1. - ²	- - -	Mrs. Wm. Eaton.
533. 1876, April 3, -	High St. Pres. Ch. Newark	Mrs. Wm. M. Halsey.
534. 1872, Feb. 3, -	2d Pres. Ch. N. Albany, Ind.	- - -
535. - - -	- - -	- - -
536. 1866, June 11, -	R. D. Ch., Syracuse, -	Mrs. H. D. Patterson.
537. - - -	- - -	- - -
538. - - -	- - -	- - -
539. 1872, Oct. 2, -	Central Cong. Ch. Brooklyn	Mrs. F. W. Phillips.
540. 1863, May 25, -	R. D. Ch. Cohoes, -	- - -
541. - - -	- - -	Mrs. Alex. Smith.
542. *1862, April 18, - ⁶⁵	- - -	Wife of a Rev. Mr. Wiedman
543. - - -	- - -	Mrs. J. G. Freeman
544. - - -	- - -	.
545. *1871, May 16, - ⁷⁵	- - -	.
546. - - -	- - -	.

NAMES.	IN, WHEN.	HOW, OR WHENCE.
547. Mary L. Rankin,⁵²⁹ - -	1862, May 2,	Confession, - -
548. Mary J. Wilcox,³²⁰ -	" "	" - -
549. Caroline H. Conrad,¹⁵⁰ -	" August 1,	" - -
550. Olive A. Vickery, -	" "	" - -
551. Mrs. Martha M. Beers, -	1863, January 30,	Meth. Ch., Aurora St. -
552, *Mrs. Margaret Hart, -	" "	" " "
553. Emily A. Winton,⁴⁸ - -	" "	Confession, - -
554. *Emily Davis, - -	" February 1,	Meth. Ch , Canoga, -
555. Almira Davis, - -	" "	" " " -
556. Mrs. Maria R. Zabriskie,	" October 30,	2d R. D. Coxsackie, -
557. Mrs. Mary A. Sibley, -	1864, February 5,	Presbyterian Ch., Ithaca, -
558. Henry A. St. John, -	" "	Confession and Baptism, -
559. Albert A. Stannard,¹⁷⁵ -	" "	" " "
560. *Mary A. Wiggin, -	" "	Crombie St. Cong.Ch. Salem
561. Edward Atwater, - -	1864, May 1,	Confession and Baptism, -
562. Ledyard J. Atwater,³⁰⁴ -	" "	Confession, - -
563. Jefferson Beardsley, - -	" "	Confession and Baptism, -
564. Harland Buckland, -	" "	" " "
565. Frederick Camp, - -	" "	Confession, - -
566. *Franklin W. Curran,²⁰² -	" "	Confession and Baptism, -
567. Martha B. Curran,²⁰² - -	" "	" " "
568. *John H. Emory, - -	" "	" " "
569. Charles E. Fiske, - -	" "	" " "
570. Jonathan G. Halsey,³⁵⁶ -	" "	Confession, - -
571. Nicoll Halsey,³⁵⁶ - -	" "	" - -
572. Mary Frances Hurd,⁵⁰¹ -	" "	" - -
573. Peter Kline, D. - -	" "	Meth, Epis. Ch., Varna. -
574. Mrs. Emeline Kline, -	" "	Pres. Ch., Harmony, -
575. Alfred C. Pope, D , - -	" "	Confession, - -
576. Sarah E. Rankin,⁵²³ -	" "	" - - -
577. Fanny M Rankin,⁵²³ -	" "	" - -
578. Mary H. St. John, -	" "	Confession and Baptism, -
579. Walter S. Schuyler,³¹⁷ -	" "	Confession, - -
580. Mrs. Elizabeth K. Stephens,	" "	Confession and Baptism, -
581. Mrs. Eliza H. S. Tappenden,	" "	Confession, - -
582. *Sarah L. Thompson, -	" "	" - -
583. Mrs. Almira Treman, -	" "	Confession and Baptism, -
584. Catherine C. Treman,⁵⁸³	" "	" " "
585. Mrs. Martha True, - -	" "	Confession, - -
586. Sarah M. True,⁵⁸⁵ -	" "	" - -
587. Charlotte L. Williams. -	" "	Confession and Baptism, -
588. Henry A. Winton,⁴⁸ -	" "	Confession. -

Out, When and How	Whither.	Remarks.
547. 1866, Jan. 3, -	Pres. Ch., Ithaca, .	. . .
548. 1861, Dec. 13, -	. . .	Mrs. A. C. Taylor.
549. 1870, Mar. 28,	Epis. Ch., Davenport, Iowa	Mrs. John Y. Lawrence.
550. 1866, May 18, -	. . .	. . .
551. - -	. . .	. . .
552. *1864, Jan. 4, -	. . .	. . .
553. - - -	. .	. . .
554. - -	. .	Mrs J. Lesley, *Brynmaur, Pa
555. - - -	. .	. . .
556. - -	. .	. . .
557. 1871, Nov. 29, -	Pres. Ch., Aurora,	Mrs. Dr Strong. .
558. - -	. .	. . .
559. - -	. .	. . .
560. *1877, May 10, -	. .	. . .
561. - -	. .	. . .
562. 1868, Feb. 27, -	. .	. . .
563. - - -	. .	. . .
564. 1865, April 20, -	Cong. Ch. Norwich,	. . .
565. - - -	. .	. . .
566. *1881, Mar. 7, - ³⁴	. .	. . .
567. - - -	. .	. . .
568. 1879, June 9, - ⁴⁰	. .	*Peoria, Ill. .
569. - - -	. .	. . .
570. - -	. .	. . .
571. 1865, Dec. 19, -	Coll. Ch., Hamilton Coll.	. . .
572. - -	. .	. . .
573. - -	. .	. . .
574. - .. -	. .	. . .
575. 1865, Dec. 19, -	Pres. Ch., Binghamton,	. . .
576. 1866, Jan. 3 -	" Ithaca, -	. . .
577. " "	" " " - .	. . .
578. 1869, July 31, -	R. D. Ch, Williamsburg,	Mrs. Jno. C. Westervelt.
579. - -	. . .	. . .
580. - -	. . .	Mrs. Philip Stephens.
581. - -	. . .	. . .
582. *1873. Nov. 6, - ³²	. . .	. . .
583. - -	. . .	Mrs Leonard Treman.
584. 1869, July 31, -	WestminsterPres.Ch.Buffalo	Mrs. J. W. Bush. -
585. - - -	. . .	Mrs. Chas. True.
586. - - -	. . .	Mrs. Wm. C. Shepard.
587. 1880, Feb. 25, -	Pres. Ch., Ithaca, -	Mrs. Chas. S. Tourtellot.
588. - - -	. . .	. . .

NAMES.	IN, WHEN.	HOW, OR WHENCE.
589. Mrs Helen C. Barton, -	1864, August 7,	Cong. Ch., Newark Valley.
590. Darius Beardsley, -	" "	Confession, - -
591. William Eaton,[470] - -	" "	Confession and Baptism, -
592. *Mrs. Isabella S. Eaton, -	" "	Confession,
593. Richard L. Goodwin, -	" "	"
594. Carrie E. Major, -	" "	" - -
595. Mrs Ann B. Morgan,[146] -	" "	" - -
596. Mrs. Amanda H. Osborn.	" "	Confession and Baptism, -
597. William P. Pope, Jr. -	" "	Confession, - -
598. Matilda S. Scribner,[607] -	" "	Confession and Baptism, -
599. Susan Smith, - - -	" "	" " "
600. Isabella L. Taber. -	" "	" " "
601. Mrs. Nancy Kenyon. -	1864, Novem'er 4,	Seneca St., Meth. Epis. Ch.,
602. Sarah E. Matthews, -	" "	Confession and Baptism, -
603. Rebecca Reed, - -	" "	" " "
604. Mrs. Mary E. Bundy, -	1865, August 4,	Aurora St. Meth.Ch.Ithaca,
605. Charlotte Mann, - -	1866, September,	R.D.Ch.,Greenwich St.N.Y
606. *Mrs. Mary W. M. Strong,	" "	" " "
607. *Mrs. Elizabeth G. Scribner,	" Novem'r 3,	15th St. Pres. Ch., N. York,
608. Gertrude E. Scribner,[607] -	" "	" " "
609. Maria Louisa Scribner,[607] -	" "	" " "
610. Matilda Bogardus, -	1867, February 2,	Confession, - -
611. Thomas F. Crane, - -	" "	1st Pres.Ch., Elizabeth, N.J.
612. Mrs. Mary E. Watkins, -	" "	Confession, - -
613. Elizabeth I. Andrus,[121] -	1867, May 5,	" - -
614. William M. Halsey,[356] -	" "	" - -
615. Minnie Major, - - -	" "	"
616. Cynthia W. Morgan,[405] -	" "	" - -
617. *Mrs Sarah D. Purdy -	" "	Presbyterian Ch., Newfield.
618. Mrs. Ellen H. Ross, -	" "	Confession, - -
619. Virginia L. Speed, -	" "	" - -
620. Ellen E. Strong,[106] -	" "	" - -
621. *Mrs. Cornelia E. S. Andrus,	1867, August 24.	2d Cong. Ch , Hartford, Ct.
622. Nicoll Halsey,[356] -	" "	Coll. Ch., Hamilton Coll.,
623. Mrs. Eliza A. Murdock. -	" "	2 Pres. Ch , Elmira,
624. Mrs. Ann E. H. Heggie.	" Nov. 2, -	Meth. Epis. Ch., Dryden,
625. Amos R. Watkins, - -	" "	Confession, - -
626. Catherine C. Bruyn, -	1868, February 4,	1st Pres. Ch., Syracuse,
627. Mrs. Maria L. S. Sawyer,	" August 1,	1st Cong. Ch., Stamford, Ct.
628. Nathaniel J. Roe, -	1869, July, 31,	R. D. Ch., Caroline, -
629. Mrs. Sarah E. G. Roe, -	" "	" " " -
630. *Mrs Margaret C. Whitbeck,	" "	" " "

Out, When and How.	Whither.	Remarks.
589. 1866, Dec. -	.	. . .
590. - -	. .	. . .
591. - - -	. .	. . .
592. *1872, Mar. 19, ³⁸	. .	*Masonville, Ia. -
593. - - -	. .	. . . .
594. - - -	. .	. . . .
595. - -	. .	Mrs. Edward J. Morgan.
596. - -	. .	. . .
597. - -	. .	. . .
598. - -	. .	Mrs. Isaac Remsen Lane.
599.	.	. . .
600. - -	. .	. . .
601. 1869, Feb. 20, -	Seneca St., M. E. Ch. Ithaca	. . .
602. 1881, March 29, -	State st., M. E. Ch. Ithaca,	Mrs. Geo. E. Buck.
603. - -	. .	. . .
604. - -	. .	. . .
605. - -	. .	. . .
606. *1868, June 23, - ⁵⁰	. .	Mrs. Dr. Strong.
607. *1875, April 5, - ⁵⁵	. .	. . .
608. - -	. .	. . .
609. 1868, Feb. 28, -	Pres. Ch., Orange N. J.	Mrs. Wm. J Nevius
610. 1870, Aug. 6, -	Pres.Ch., Kalamazoo,Mich.	. . .
611. - -	. .	. . .
612. 1876, Feb. 28, -	Pres. Ch., Ithaca, -	Mrs. Amos Watkins, -
613. - -	. .	Mrs. J. Arthur Anderson.
614. 1876, April 3, -	High st. Pres. Ch. Newark	. .
615. - -	. .	Mrs. H. S. Burnell.
616. - -	. .	. . .
617. *1879, Jan. 7, - ⁽⁵	. .	Mrs. Ebenezer Purdy, -
618. - -	. .	. . .
619. 1870, Feb. 15, -	Pres. Ch., Watkins, -	. . .
620. 1871, Nov. 29, -	Pres. Ch., Aurora, -	. . .
621. *1876, Dec. 14, - ⁵⁰	. .	. . .
622. - -	. .	. . .
623. - -	. .	. . .
624. - -	. .	Mrs. Jas. M. Heggie.
625. 1877. -	dis. by classis, - -	. . .
626. - -	. .	. . .
627. - -	. .	Mrs. Sam. D. Sawyer.
628. 1874, Dec. 17, -	Plymouth Ch.,LansingMich.	. . .
629. " "	" " "	. . .
630. *1875. Mar. 19, - ⁵³	. .	wf. of Rev.Mr. J. Whitbeck.

NAMES.	IN, WHEN.	HOW, OR WHENCE.
631. Maria L. Whitbeck,[30] -	1869, July 31,	R. D. Ch., Caroline.
632. Thomas M. Strong,[606] -	" "	Confession, - -
633. Susan H. Atwater, -	" Nov. 6,	" - - -
634. *Mrs. Mary Wiggin, - -	" "	Cong. Ch. Salem, Mass.
635. Dudley M. Finch, -	1870, January 29,	Presbyterian Ch., Ithaca,
636. Mary E Terry, - -	" "	Confession, - -
637. H. W. Van Wageman, -	" "	Middle R. D. Ch. Brooklyn
638. Ada M. Stoddard, - -	" August 6,	Confession, -
639. Catherine C. Andrus,[419]	1871, February 4,	" - -
640. Caroline H. Andrus,[419] -	" "	" - -
641. Mary C. Atwater,[361] -	" "	" - -
642. Julius C. Cable, - -	" "	" - -
643. Mrs. Harriet E. Carter, -	" "	" - -
644. Catherine K. Church,[350] -	" "	" - -
645. Andrew P. Fairman, -	" "	" - -
646. Sarah A. Kenyon, - -	" "	" - -
647. Adeline Ostrander, -	" "	" - -
648. Mary E. Roe,[2] - -	" "	" - -
649. Mrs. Julia D. Thompson,	" "	" - -
650. Mary E. Tompkins, -	" "	" - -
651. Kate Andrus,[21] - -	1871, April 1,	" - -
652. Helen L. Andrus,[21] -	" "	" - -
653. Mary T. Andrus,[419] -	" "	" - -
654. Frank Josephine Atwater, -	" "	" - -
655. William A. Church,[350] -	" "	" - -
656. *Hugh Stanley Halsey,[356]	" "	" - -
657. Minerva McChain,[734] -	" July 1,	" - -
658. Emma McChain,[734] -	" "	" - -
659. Lizzie Stephens,[380] -	" "	" - -
660. Margaret S. Whitbeck,[30] -	" "	R. D. Ch., Flatbush. -
661. Fred. L. Wick, - -	" "	Confession, - -
662. *Mrs. Susan Heath, - -	" "	Pres. Ch., Ithaca. -
663. William F. Major, -	" "	Confession, - -
664. Mrs. Amelia S. Eldred, -	" Sept. 30,	Presbyterian Ch., Waverly,
665. Ella Betts, - - -	1873, -	Aurora st M. E. Ch., -
666. Wm. M Eaton,[501] - -	" "	Confession, - -
667. Chas. S. Harman, -	" "	Cong. Ch. Blue Island, Ill.
668. Waterman T. Hewett, E. -	" "	" Amherst College
669. Mrs. Joanna L. Hunt, -	" "	" Owego, - -
670. Orange P. Hyde, D.! -	" "	" Prairie du Chien
671. William Kinne, E -	" "	" Yale College Ch
672. Mrs. Phebe Adams Kinne,	" "	3d Cong. Ch., New Haven,

Out, When and How.	Whither.	Remarks.
631. 1875, April 14, -	Presbyterian Ch., Ithaca, -	- - - -
632. 1871, Nov. 29,	Presbyterian Ch., Aurora,	- - - -
633. - -	- - -	Mrs. James E. Henriques.
634. *1874, Jan. 2,	- - -	.
635. - -	- - -	.
636. - -	- - -	Mrs. John A. Rea.
637. 1871, Dec. 2, -	R. D. Ch., New York. -	- - - -
638. 1872, Oct. 31,	Pres. Ch., Ithaca, -	- - -
639. -		- - -
640. - -	- - -	- - -
641. - -	- - -	- - -
642. - -	- - -	- - -
643. - -	Cortland, -	Mrs. Chas. Carter.
644. - -	- - -	Mrs. Fred. L. Wick.
645. - -	- - -	- - -
646. - -	- - -	Mrs. Albert N. Ackley.
647. 1877, April 19, -	Pres. Ch., Ithaca, -	- - -
648. 1874, Dec. 16, -	PlymouthCh.,Lansing,Mich	- - -
649. - -	- - -	Mrs. Sewall Thompson, jr.
650. - -	- - -	- - -
651. - -	- - -	Mrs. Clarence Beebe.
652. - -	- - -	- - -
653. - -	- - -	- - -
654. 1874, Nov. 25, -	Pres. Ch., Chicago, -	- - -
655. -	- - -	- - -
656. *1874, Oct. 17, - 20	- - -	- - -
657. - -	- - -	- - -
658. - -	- - -	Mrs. Waterman T. Hewett.
659. - -	- - -	- - -
660. 1875, April 14, -	Pres. Ch., Ithaca, -	- - -
661. - -	- - -	- - -
662. *1877, May 15, - 77	- - -	- - -
663. - -	- - -	- - -
664. - -	- - -	Mrs. Horace Eldred.
665. - -	- - -	Mrs. G. P. Serviss. -
666. - -	- - -	- - -
667. 1877, April 24,	- - -	- - -
668. - -	- - -	. .
669. - -	- - -	Mrs. Warren Hunt.
670. - -	- - -	. .
671. - -	- - -	. .
672- - -	- - -	. . .

NAMES.	IN. WHEN.	HOW, OR WHENCE.
673. Mrs. Mary L. W. Lacy,	1873, -	Cong. Ch., Groton, -
674. *Samuel Love, - -	" "	Seneca St., Meth. Epis. Ch.,
675. *Mrs. Mary Love, - -	" "	" " "
676. Mrs. Mary L. McChain,	" "	Presbyterian Ch., Ithaca. -
677. Caroline W. McChain, -	" "	14th St. Pres. Ch., N. York.
678. Chas. W. Major, - -	" "	Confession, - -
679. Mrs. Ann Matthews. - -	" "	Congregational Ch.,Candor.
680. Mrs. Margaret H. Hind,	1874. January 2,	R. D. Ch., Brooklyn. -
681. Julia E. Kimball,[97] - -	" "	Confession, - -
682. *John J. Mills,	" "	" - -
683. Tracy Peck, E..	" "	" - -
684. Mrs. Tracy Peck, - -	" "	Plymouth Con.Ch.Brooklyn
685. Mrs. Susan J. Taylor,[98] -	" "	Presbyterian Ch., Ithaca.
686. Eugene L. Ware,	" "	3d Cong.Ch..San Francisco,
687. *Evan W. Evans, -	1874. February 15,	Cong. Ch., Marietta, Ohio,
688. Mrs. Helen C. Evans,	" "	" " "
689. Alice Evans,[99]	" "	Pres. Ch., Franklin,
690. Archibald H. Bill,	1874, April 5,	" Geneva, -
691. Mrs. Francis Hintermister,	" "	Confession. - -
692. Clara Atwater,[300] -	1874. October 5,	" -
693. Kate M. Beers,[1] -	" "	" - -
694. Susan B. Scribner,[2] -	" "	" - -
695. Mrs. Mary A. R. Hall,	1875, January 9,	R. D. Ch., Farmer Village,
696. Franklin M. Kendall,	" "	Presbyterian Ch., Attica. -
697. Mrs. Harriet Kimball, -	" "	Congregational Ch. Elmira,
698. Samuel J. Parker, -	" "	Presbyterian Ch., Ithaca. -
699. Mrs. R. L. F. Parker, -	" "	" " "
700. Henry W. Sackett,[*] -	" "	Baptist Ch , Ithaca,
701. *George Whiton, E.,[202]	" "	Presbyterian Ch., Ithaca, -
702. Mrs. Sylvia N. Whiton, -	" "	" " "
703. Kate L. Whiton,[203] -	" "	- - -
704. Henry D. Winans,	" "	Pres. Ch.. Newark, N. J. -
705. Mrs. Lucy L. Winans. -	" "	" " -
706. Rhoda B. Manning.	1875. April 4,	Confession.
707. Harriet Marsh, -	" "	Presbyterian Ch., Ithaca,
708. Nathan W. Barber. -	" 28.	Cong. Ch. Newark Valley.
709. Mrs. Fanny Barber. - -	"	Meth. Epis. Ch.. Danby.
710. Cynthia M. Whiton,[204] -	" "	Presbyterian Ch., Ithaca, -
711. Mrs. Lucy Lemon Gay, -	" Sept. 12,	" " Waverly,
712. *Harriet Clough, -	1876, January 4,	" " Nunda,
713. Louise M. Lacy,[674] - -	" "	Congregational Ch., Groton,
714. Mrs. Mary St J. Westervelt,	" "	R.D.Ch.,Bed.Av.,Brooklyn

Out, When and How.	Whither.	Remarks.
631. 1875, April 14, -	Presbyterian Ch., Ithaca, -	- - -
632. 1871, Nov. 29,	Presbyterian Ch., Aurora,	- - -
633. - -	- - -	Mrs. James E. Henriques.
634. *1874, Jan. 2,	- - -	.
635. - -	- - -	. .
636. - -	- - -	Mrs. John A. Rea.
637. 1871, Dec. 2, -	R. D. Ch., New York. -	- - -
638. 1872, Oct. 31,	Pres. Ch., Ithaca, -	- - -
639. -	- - -	- - -
640. - -	- - -	- - -
641. - -	- - -	- - -
642. - -	- - -	- - -
643. - -	Cortland, -	Mrs. Chas. Carter.
644. - -	- - -	Mrs. Fred. L. Wick.
645. - -	- - -	- - -
646. - -	- - -	Mrs. Albert N. Ackley.
647. 1877, April 19, -	Pres. Ch., Ithaca, -	- - -
648. 1874, Dec. 16, -	PlymouthCh.,Lansing,Mich	- - -
649. - -	- - -	Mrs. Sewall Thompson. jr.
650. -	- - -	- - -
651. - -	- - -	Mrs. Clarence Beebe.
652. - -	- - -	- - -
653. . -	- - -	- - -
654. 1874, Nov. 25. -	Pres. Ch., Chicago, -	- - -
655. - -	- - -	- - -
656. *1874, Oct. 17, - 20	- - -	- - -
657. - -	- - -	- - -
658. - -	- - -	Mrs. Waterman T. Hewett.
659. - -	- - -	- - -
660. 1875, April 14, -	Pres. Ch., Ithaca, -	- - -
661. - -	- - -	- - -
662. *1877, May 15, - 77	- - -	- - -
663. - -	- - -	- - -
664. - -	- - -	Mrs. Horace Eldred.
665. - -	- - -	Mrs. G. P. Serviss. -
666. - -	- - -	- - -
667. 1877, April 24,	- - -	- - -
668. - -	- - -	. .
669. - -	- - -	Mrs. Warren Hunt.
670. - -	- - -	. .
671. - -	- - -	. .
672. - -	- - -	. .

NAMES.	IN. WHEN.	HOW, OR WHENCE.
673. Mrs. Mary L. W. Lacy,	1873, -	Cong. Ch., Groton, -
674. *Samuel Love, - -	" "	Seneca St., Meth. Epis. Ch.,
675. *Mrs. Mary Love, - -	" "	" " "
676. Mrs. Mary L. McChain,	" "	Presbyterian Ch., Ithaca. -
677. Caroline W. McChain, -	" "	14th St. Pres. Ch., N. York.
678. Chas. W. Major, - -	" "	Confession, - -
679. Mrs. Ann Matthews. - -	" "	Congregational Ch.,Candor.
680. Mrs. Margaret H. Hind,	1874. January 2,	R. D. Ch., Brooklyn. -
681. Julia E. Kimball,[07] - -	" "	Confession, - -
682. *John J. Mills,	" "	" - -
683. Tracy Peck, E..	" "	" -
684. Mrs. Tracy Peck, - -	" "	Plymouth Con.Ch.Brooklyn
685. Mrs. Susan J. Taylor,[12] -	" "	Presbyterian Ch., Ithaca.
686. Eugene L. Ware,	" "	3d Cong.Ch..San Francisco,
687. *Ivan W. Evans, -	1874. February 15,	Cong. Ch., Marietta, Ohio,
688. Mrs. Helen C. Evans,	" "	" " "
689. Alice Evans.[157]	" "	Pres. Ch., Franklin,
690. Archibald H. Bill,	1874, April 5,	" Geneva, -
691. Mrs. Francis Hintermister,	" "	Confession. - -
692. Clara Atwater.[301] -	1874. October 5,	"
693. Kate M. Beers,[43] -	" "	" - -
694. Susan B. Scribner,[07] -	" "	" - -
695. Mrs. Mary A. R. Hall.	1875, January 9,	R. D. Ch., Farmer Village,
696. Franklin M. Kendall,	" "	Presbyterian Ch., Attica. -
697. Mrs. Harriet Kimball,	" "	Congregational Ch. Elmira,
698. Samuel J. Parker, -	" "	Presbyterian Ch., Ithaca. -
699. Mrs. R. L. F. Parker, -	"	" " "
700. Henry W. Sackett, ' -	"	Baptist Ch , Ithaca, -
701. 'George Whiton, E.,[302]	" "	Presbyterian Ch., Ithaca, -
702. Mrs. Sylvia N. Whiton, -	"	" " "
703. Kate L. Whiton,[301] -	" "	- - -
704. Henry D. Winans,	" "	Pres. Ch.. Newark, N. J. -
705. Mrs. Lucy L. Winans. -	" "	" " "
706. Rhoda B. Manning,	1875. April 1,	Confession. -
707. Harriet Marsh, -	" "	Presbyterian Ch., Ithaca,
708. Nathan W. Barber.	" 28.	Cong. Ch. Newark Valley.
709. Mrs. Fanny Barber. - -	"	Meth. Epis. Ch.. Danby. - -
710. Cynthia M. Whiton,[301]	" "	Presbyterian Ch., Ithaca, -
711. Mrs. Lucy Lemon Gay, -	" Sept. 12,	" " Waverly.
712. *Harriet Clough, -	1876, January 4,	" " Nunda, -
713. Louise M. Lacy,[634] - -	" "	Congregational Ch., Groton,
714. Mrs. Mary St J. Westervelt,	" "	R.D.Ch.,Bed.Av.,Brooklyn

Out, When and How.	Whither.	Remarks.
673.		
674. *1881, April 9,		
675. *1889, Feb. 6,		
676.		Mrs. Geo. McChain,.
677.		
678.		
679.		
680.		
681. 1879, Dec. 14,	Cong. Ch., Philadelphia.	Mrs. Chas. Martin.
682.		*Australia.
683. 1880, Oct. 27,	Yale Coll. Ch., Conn.	
684. " "	" " "	
685.		Mrs. Jas. B. Taylor.
686. 1878, Oct.	Philips Ch., S. Boston, Mass	
687. *1874, May 22,		
688. 1878.	Troy.	
689.		Mrs. Charles Francis.
690. 1874, Sept. 27,	Central Pres. Ch. Auburn.	
691.		
692.		
693.		Mrs. James Rogers.
694.		Mrs. E. J. Morgan, Jr.
695.		Mrs. Edwin M. Hall.
696.		
697. 1879, Dec. 14,	Cong. Ch. Philadelphia.	Mrs. Orison Kimball.
698.		M. D.
699.		
700.		
701. *1878. Nov. 25,		
702.		
703.		
704.		
705.		
706.		
707. 1878, Oct.	Pres. Ch., Ithaca,	
708.		
709.		
710.		
711.		Mrs. Chas. W. Gay.
712. *1876, Aug.		*Nunda.
713.		
714.		Mrs. Jno. C. Westervelt.

	NAMES.	IN, WHEN.	HOW, OR WHENCE.
715.	Mahlon H. Brown,	1875, April 2,	Presbyterian Ch., Ithaca,
716.	Mrs. Mary M. Brown,	" "	" " "
717.	Charlotte Case,⁷³³	" "	Confession,
718.	Nellie Case,⁷³³	" "	"
719.	Albert M. Hull,	" "	Presbyterian Ch., Ithaca,
720.	Mrs. Marg. V. Hull,	" "	" " "
721. *Mrs. Olive G. Pratt,	" "	Congregational Ch., Chelsea
722.	James Seaman	" "	Confession and Baptism,
723.	Mrs. Marg. Seaman,	" "	Seneca St., Meth. Epis. Ch.
724.	Mrs. Louise Slocum,	" "	Congregational Ch., Danby,
725.	Walter J. Terry,⁴⁰²	" "	Confession,
726.	Gazena Visscher,	" "	Presbyterian Ch., Ithaca,
727.	Mrs. Mary Wood,	" "	" Cortland,
728.	Edwin J. Burritt,	1876, June 28,	" Ithaca,
729.	Mrs. Louise Burritt,	" "	" "
730. *Wm. B. Foote,	" "	" Waterloo,
731.	Josie C. Nichols,	" "	
732.	Wm. J. Storms,⁷⁴²	" "	Presbyterian Ch., Ithaca,
733.	Mrs. Hannah L. Storms,⁷⁴⁶	" "	" " "
734.	George McChain,	" "	" " "
735.	George Kinney,	1876, October 1,	1st Cong. Ch , Oberlin, O.,
736.	Mrs. Mary L. P. Kinney,	" "	" " "
737.	Harriet S. Kinney,⁷³⁰	" "	" " "
738.	Mary M. Kinney.⁷³⁰	" "	" " "
739.	Geo. H. Northrup,	" "	Confession,
740.	Mrs. Addie Northrup,	" "	"
741.	Mrs. Ann Rounseville,	" "	Cong. Ch., Mott's Corners,
742. *Thomas Storms,	" "	Presbyterian Ch., Ithaca,
743. *Mrs. Lavina Storms,	" "	" " "
744.	Louise E. Storms,⁷³²	" "	" " "
745.	Mrs. Adelia C. Foote.	1877, January 7,	" " "
746.	Mrs. Isabella A. Burdick,	1877, March 28,	" " "
747	Kittie Saxton,	" "	Confession,
748.	A. J. Madison,	" Oct. 7,	By Letter,
749.	Mrs. A. J. Madison,	" "	"
750.	Florence F. Parker,⁷⁰⁸	" "	Presbyterian Ch., Ithaca,
751.	Rosabella E. Burdick,⁷⁴⁶	1878, January,	Confession,
752.	Frederica Andrus,⁴¹⁹	" April 7,	"
753.	Mrs. Sarah Jane Case,	" "	"
754.	Mary E. Crozier,	" "	"
755.	Effie Custeed,	" "	"
756.	Kate Clark Evans,⁶⁸⁷	" "	"

Out, When and How.	Whither.	Remarks.
715. 1880, Feb 22, -	PlymouthCong.Ch.Syracuse	M. D.
716. " "	" " "	-
717. - -	- - -	Mrs. Chas. C. Prime.
718.	- -	
719.	- - -	-
720. -	- -	- -
721. *1879, Jan. - 74	-	*Elmira. -
722. - - -	- -	
723. -	- -	- -
724. -	-	Mrs. Chas. H. Slocum.
725.	- - -	- - -
726. -	- - -	- - -
727.	- - -	- - -
728.	- -	
729. - -	- -	- -
730. *1879, July 4, -	- -	-
731. 1881, Feb. 9, -	2d Pres. Ch. Rochester.	Mrs. Post.
732. - - -	- - -	
733. - - -	- - -	
734. - - -	- -	
735. - - -	- - -	
736. -	- - -	
737.	- - -	- - -
738. 1880, Feb. 11,	Cong. Ch. Ann Arbor, Mich	Mrs. Chas. N. Jones.
739. - - -	- - -	
740. -	- -	
741. - - -		- -
742. *1878, May 9,	-	- - -
743. *1880, March 29,	- - -	- -
744. - - -	- -	-
745. - - -	- - -	Mrs. Wm. J. P. Foote.
746. - - -	- -	-
747. - - -	- -	
748. 1878, Oct.	Pres. Ch , Binghamton,	-
749. "	" "	- -
750.	- - -	-
751.	- - -	Mrs. Fred H. Miller.
752.	- -	- -
753. - -	- -	
754. - - -	- -	-
755. 1879, Mar. 31, -	2d Pres. Ch. Altoona, Pa.	
756. - - -	- - -	- - -

	NAMES.	IN, WHEN.	HOW, OR WHENCE.
757.	J. Thornton Osmond, -	1878, April 7,	Confession, -
758.	Louisa St. John, - -	" "	"
759,	Carrie K. Storms,⁷³² -	" "	"
760.	Mrs. Dora Teed, - -	" "	"
761.	Fanny Wenona Williams,⁴⁷⁵	" "	" - -
762.	Mary Gavina Hungerford,⁴⁷⁹	" "	" -
763.	Anna M. Livermore, -	1879, March 31,	2d Pres. Ch , Geneva, -
764.	Mrs. Linda M. Sherwood,	" "	Confession, -
765.	Ella Williams, - -	" "	" - -
766.	Mary Euphemia Woodruff,	" "	" - -
767.	George Beardsley, D., -	1879, July 4,	Congregational Ch , Danby.
768.	Mrs. Mary Beardsley, -	" "	" " " -
769.	Lewis Beardsley,⁷⁷ -	" "	" " "
770.	Henry Wegman, -	" "	- -
771.	Mrs. Julia Wegman, -	" "	- - -
772.	Mrs. Louise S. Houghton,⁷¹	1879, October 5,	Pres. Ch., Norwood, N.J.
773.	Mary Houghton, ⁷⁷² -	1879. July 4,	" " "
774.	Augustus S. Houghton,⁷⁷² -	" "	M.E.Ch., Atlanticville N. J.
775.	Elihu Russell Houghton,⁷⁷²	" "	R. D. Ch., Piermont, N. J.
776.	Wm Arnon Henry, - -	" Novem'r 23.	Confession, - -

39

Out, When and How.	Whither.	Remarks
757.		
758.		
759.		
760.		
761.		
762.		
763.		
764.		Mrs. Chas. R. Sherwood.
765.		
766.		
767.		
768.		
769.		
770.		
771.		
772.		
773.		
774.		
775.		
776.		

☞ In numbers 107, 159, 225, 226, 227 and 254 insert 223 after the name in the first column. In number 409, 4th column, read, *1878, July 4. ×.

Whole number of names,   -   -   -   776

Twice mentioned,   -   24

Whole number of members,   -   -   752

Index.

INDEX TO MARRIED NAMES.

www.ingramcontent.com/pod-product-compliance
Lightning Source LLC
Chambersburg PA
CBHW021522090426
42739CB00007B/743